SOFTWARE REFLECTED

Software Reflected

The Socially Responsible Programming
of Our Computers

Robert Laurence Baber

1982

NORTH-HOLLAND PUBLISHING COMPANY
AMSTERDAM · NEW YORK · OXFORD

ISBN: 0 444 86372 9

PUBLISHED BY:

NORTH-HOLLAND PUBLISHING COMPANY
AMSTERDAM · NEW YORK · OXFORD

SOLE DISTRIBUTORS FOR THE U.S.A. AND CANADA:

ELSEVIER SCIENCE PUBLISHING COMPANY, INC.
52 VANDERBILT AVENUE
NEW YORK, N.Y. 10017

Library of Congress Cataloging in Publication Data

Baber, Robert Laurence.
    Software reflected.

    Bibliography: p.
    Includes index.
    1. Electronic digital computers--Programming--
Social aspects. I. Title.
QA76.6.B26   303.4'834   82-3491
ISBN 0-444-86372-9   AACR2

PRINTED IN THE NETHERLANDS

Acknowledgments

Many of the ideas expressed in this book were formulated during the course of discussions with my wife, Ursula. Only by trying to explain to her, a layman in computer matters, what is wrong with the way we currently go about trying to develop software did it become evident to me how difficult it is for a non-computerite to believe that the software situation of today could be as bad as it really is. Her efforts to comprehend the nature of the process by which we design and develop software, our trials and tribulations as well as the causes of our current difficulties have contributed significantly to the arguments presented in this book.

I am deeply indebted to my many past and present consulting clients, teachers, business colleagues and personal friends who have, in the course of time, contributed to the formation of the ideas contained in this book. They have also contributed, unintentionally, much of the anecdotal and narrative material in chapter 2.

My thanks go to Roger M. Pickering and Henry F. Sherwood for reviewing a draft of this book and contributing many helpful comments. To Drs. Willem Dijkhuis of the North-Holland Publishing Company I am grateful for encouragement, constructive critism and an observation on the connection between mathematics and the development of a scientific field (see the introductory comments in chapter 3).

Cartographic credit is due to my daughter, Ingrid, for preparing the map of the land of the Ret Up Moc.

I am also grateful to the many computer hardware engineers who have contributed to the development of microcomputer systems. Without such a system, the preparation of the draft of this book would have taken much longer and would have involved much tedious effort. I am very glad that such systems became available to individual authors at home before I started to write this book.

Thanks are due also, of course, to those who prepared the word processing software used in the preparation of the draft of this book. But I must note, unfortunately, that the quality of this software was not quite up to the standards met by the hardware. While the errors in that software were minor and did not preclude productive use of the system, they were more than cosmetic defects -- which brings me to the subject of this book.

Robert Laurence Baber
6380 Bad Homburg v.d.H.
Federal Republic of Germany
June 1981

Contents

The Land of the Ret Up Moc, ca. 2400 B.C.

Chapter 0

Prologue: the land of Moc

It is better to be unborn than untaught, for ignorance is the root of misfortune.

Plato (ca. 428 B.C.–ca. 348 B.C.)

He who knoweth not what he ought to know is a brute beast among men.

Pythagoras (ca. 572 B.C.–ca. 497 B.C.)

Around 2500 B.C. the land of Moc was one of the more advanced societies in the cradle of civilization, the Middle East. While Moc's economy was based primarily on agriculture, its growing internal and foreign trade was already of considerable importance. It had reached such a stage of development that a number of closely interacting cities and towns had arisen; the largest of these had a population of some 100,000. Hierarchically organized governmental and religious bureaucracies of moderate size had been established and two or three centers of learning appear to have existed.

The construction of the towns and cities over the years had given rise to a significant building industry and to a certain demand for architectural and civil engineering services. The suppliers of these services prepared themselves for their careers by attending a specialized school where they studied arithmetic, geometry, elementary algebra, a rudimentary form of materials science, something we might today call project management and several other relevant subjects. After completing this three year formal academic program, the newly graduated architect or engineer worked under the close supervision of an experienced professional for another one to two years. Upon passing an examination, he was then licensed to practice his craft.

1

In 2480 B.C. a development occurred which was to have a tremendous impact on Mocsian society. A small group of civil engineering teachers at the most advanced institution worked out a new technique for designing a building. Key elements of this technique were several new structural geometries and the application of a newly developed mathematical method to the problem of calculating stresses in complicated structures of load carrying elements. Using this new technique, multistory buildings could be designed and built which were much larger than any built before. Perhaps even more importantly, the proper application of the new technique could reduce construction costs to about one tenth of their previous levels.

Not surprisingly, this unexpected new development was followed by a sudden, sharp increase in the demand for new construction. Larger versions of traditional types of buildings (houses, apartments, shops, offices, sports arenas, etc.) were in great demand. Many peasants who had previously lived in self-made mud and straw huts could now afford housing of a type previously available only to the middle and upper classes. The political leaders decided to build several huge monuments to the glory of Mocsian society. Religious leaders commissioned important new structures for use as temples and as astrological and astronomical observatories.

The application of this new technology was not without its dark side, however. The sharply increased demand for architectural and civil engineering services greatly exceeded the capacity of the trained Mocsian professionals. In order to train greater numbers of these professionals, the capacity of the training centers would have had to be increased. But the economic pressures of the market place had just the opposite effect – some of the teachers left academia to earn even more money as practicing professionals and few, if any, of the new graduates went into teaching.

Compounding the problems was the fact that the already trained professionals were not really able to understand and apply the new techniques satisfactorily. Additional training, especially in geometry and a new branch of mathematics, was necessary. Few practitioners were inclined and in a position to take leave of their work for six months in order to learn these subjects.

Economic forces soon caused the gap between supply and demand to be bridged. By about 2420 B.C., the following state of quasi equilibrium had been reached.

Suppliers of building materials had developed short courses (about three weeks in length) which more or less successfully conveyed some of the essentials of the new engineering techniques. A few already trained professionals attended these courses at first, but the majority of the participants were either completely new to the building industry or had previously been laborers on construction teams. These courses were especially popular among apprentice sod carriers, who soon realized that preparing construction plans in a cool office was less strenuous and more rewarding work than carrying large volumes of sod in the heat of Mocsian summer.

Other groups of persons involved in the building industry, including a few trained architects and civil engineers, developed design kits. These kits included
- a design handbook,
- sample forms, drawings and plans,
- special purpose slide rules,
- preprinted graphs and diagrams for calculating stresses in beams, walls, floors and ceilings,
- drawing templates and graphic tools,
- designers' checklists,
- a book summarizing the theories underlying the new design technique and a variety of other similar tools and design aids, some of which were of dubious value. Characteristic of the written materials in these kits was the extensive use of pictorial information, for a significant fraction of the new designers was barely literate.

Armed with such a design kit, most of those who completed one of the three week courses were able to prepare construction plans for new buildings. Because they did not, however, really understand the theory underlying their designs, minor catastrophes were common. About 30% of all newly designed buildings collapsed during construction. Often, minor but required features were forgotten in the plans and post-construction rework was usually necessary.

Even after taking these problems into account, construction costs were still only a fraction of what they would have been using the older methods. No one, therefore, seriously considered or suggested reverting to the old ways. Loss of life of the occupants of completed buildings and of other members of the public was actually rare, because the buildings collapsed only during or immediately after construction. There was clearly a net benefit to society of using the new design technique and so its use not only continued, but grew rapidly.

To combat the problem of loss of life of laborers when buildings under construction suddenly collapsed, elaborate testing schemes were worked out. Certain stages of construction were identified as pre-critical ones. When a building reached such a stage of construction, the site was cleared and the structure tested by loading it with sand and rubble. Various arrangements of cranes, winches and ropes were used to bring the loads into place so that laborers were not in danger should the structure collapse. After construction was complete, a similar final test was conducted. A very considerable part of the total cost and time required to construct the typical building could be attributed to these testing procedures, but without them, no construction foreman was willing to assume responsibility for the lives of his laborers. Some small organizations even supplied a variety of testing kits, similar to the design kits described earlier.

Nevertheless, tempers and frustration with cost overruns, missed schedules and the generally poor quality of buildings ran high. In order to protect themselves from legal claims, the designers began to write a standard legend on each drawing or plan delivered to their clients. This legend, which had long been an unsolved mystery in our study of the Mocsian culture, has only recently been successfully translated as follows:

DISCLAIMER

These building plans are supplied on an "as-is" basis. The designer makes no guarantees, warranties or representations that these plans are suitable for any particular purpose, that they are correct or that a building constructed using them will satisfy any particular needs of the purchaser. The designer agrees to supply a replacement copy of any part(s) of these plans which was (were) illegible at the time of purchase. Otherwise, he accepts no liability of any kind.

The purchaser of these plans should note that good construction practice dictates that appropriate tests be conducted at the several pre-critical stages of construction as well as upon completion of the building and that normal precautions be taken to safeguard the lives of construction laborers.

The above translation has, however, been questioned by some scholars. They point out that it is in conflict with our knowledge of Mocsian commercial practice and law. In Moc, a long commercial tradition required that the seller repair or replace goods found to be defective or that he refund the purchase price if the goods could not be made to fulfill their intended purpose. Suppliers of services accepted a similar obligation. This tradition was well established and was anchored in Mocsian commercial law. If the above translation of the disclaimer legend is in fact correct, the new breed of building designers constituted the only known exception to this long commercial tradition.

Recent excavations in Moc have even turned up small stone tablets with the disclaimer legend engraved in reverse. It has been postulated that these tablets were used then as we use rubber stamps today.

Between 2420 and 2400 B.C., the teachers and their professionally trained assistants refined the new technique, with the result that construction costs declined even more and demand for new construction rose to still higher levels. As a consequence, not even the rather large number of "three week wonders with design kits" (as the professionally trained designers contemptuously labelled their minimally trained colleagues) could cope with the demand for plans for new buildings. Some relief was obtained by using one set of plans for many buildings (a practice commonly called "off-shelving"), but individual tastes and differing requirements limited the extent to which this approach could be used.

Some larger trading and other organizations set up small staffs of designers they had recruited from among their employees. Each of these new designers was sent to an abbreviated version of the three week courses and upon his return was given his own design kit. While these internal designers were reasonably effective at designing additions and modifications to their organization's existing buildings, they were generally less successful in designing completely new structures. Cost overruns, construction delays and collapses of partially constructed buildings seemed to occur more often when structures they designed were being built. Members of these internal design staffs generally worked under less time pressure than their independent colleagues. Because they were usually paid less than independent designers could earn, the more ambitious and the better designers did not usually remain in the employ of a large organization for any really significant length of time.

Some designers joined together and formed small design teams or organizations. These became popularly known as "design houses", a kind of play on words which is more effective in the original Mocsian than it is in translation. Some of these design houses developed a variation of "off-shelving": they accumulated libraries of standard plans for parts of buildings (rooms, tracts, entire floors, etc.). Such plans for parts of buildings could be combined more or less arbitrarily as needed to make up a set of plans for a new building. This approach was called "modularized off-shelving" and became something of a craze.

Some design houses had one or two professionally trained designers on their teams. These professionals usually contributed considerably to the effectiveness of the designers with less formal training. Most of these design houses enjoyed a good reputation and were very successful.

Despite the development of improved methods, the designers could not keep up with the growth in demand for their services. By 2400 B.C., the situation had reached the point that a prospective builder had to wait about two years for a set of plans to be prepared – even for plans for a relatively simple building. The overall quality of the designs being produced was not really improving. While the "three week wonders" were learning from their experience, more complex and more ambitious projects were being initiated. Because their specific experience with previous designs was only of limited applicability to typical new projects and because their understanding of theoretical geometry and statics was so limited, they were not successful in their attempts to improve the fundamental quality of their designs. In fact, the collapse rate (the ratio of collapses to new building starts) was actually increasing. According to official government statistics, it reached a new high of 34.9% in 2400 B.C.

Except for the "three week wonders", who were convinced that the current situation was Adad's will (and wasn't really all that bad anyway), no one was really satisfied with the state of affairs in the Mocsian building industry in 2400 B.C. Several studies were conducted, the results of which were somewhat contradictory. Most of the studies tried to compare and evaluate proposed ways of improving the situation, rather than to identify the causes of the problems. An almost unbelievable number of new tricks, methods, procedures, etc. was invented and promulgated. Some were useless. Others were based on incorrect assumptions and were actually harmful. But many definitely were valuable and effective; the only problem was that the less well trained designers could not understand these new methods well enough to apply them meaningfully. The relatively few professionals could, and many of them did, apply these methods successfully, but the overall effect on the industry as a whole was disappointingly small.

The professional designers (about 10% of all designers in 2400 B.C.) were particularly annoyed by the fact that much of their time was spent correcting or trying to overcome the effects of the mistakes perpetrated by their less thoroughly trained colleagues. Upon his arrival one day at the scene of an especially catastrophic collapse, a particularly eloquent professional was overheard to remark in disgust, "rubbish in, rubble out". The "rubbish in" to which he referred was, of course, the set of plans prepared by a "three week wonder". The "rubble out" was an immense pile of rubble which then occupied the site. He estimated that it would take 1,000 laborers and 200 draft animals one year to remove the rubble and to clear the site in preparation for the next construction attempt.

The professionally trained designers were worried about the long term effect these problems were certain to have upon their reputation and social standing. They were also frustrated by the small – in their view – difference between their earnings and those of the "three week wonders". They were convinced that the collapse rate was closely correlated with the professional qualifications of the designer preparing the plans. Their professional guild had conducted a few surveys, the results of which, to no one's surprise, confirmed this contention. Purchasers were generally willing to pay more for plans prepared by a professional designer, but in the eyes of the professionals this difference was much less than was warranted by the reduced risk of collapse. The official government statistics on collapse rates did not distinguish between buildings designed by the two groups so were of no relevance to discussions of this issue.

A few enlightened leaders in Mocsian society agreed by and large with the professional designers. They, too, were convinced that a certain body of theoretical knowledge was very useful to anyone practicing the craft of designing buildings. In the long run, the professional education of prospective designers was clearly of considerable economic value.

The difficulties were great, however, in inducing a transition to the ideal situation in which most, if not all, designers would complete a professional training program before embarking upon their careers. First, the capacity of the professional training institutions would have to be increased substantially. The problem of financing this increase was a very

difficult one. Then there was the question of how to select those experienced professionals who should leave their practices in order to help
teach the next generation of designers. Even if they could be selected, it
was not at all clear how they could be motivated to give up interesting
and lucrative careers in favor of an uncertain future in teaching. And
even if that problem could be solved, there still remained the task of
inducing prospective designers to postpone substantial earnings for some
three years while they received a professional education.

Neither the professional guild nor the few enlightened leaders of
similar opinion were in a position to solve the problem of financing a
major expansion of the professional training institutions. Either a much
larger group from the private sector or the political leadership of the
country would have to be convinced of the desirability of these contem-
plated changes if sufficient funds were to be mobilized for this purpose.
In view of the fact that the productivity of Mocsian society and the
standard of living of its citizens were at an all-time high, it was essentially
impossible to generate any large scale, popular support for an expensive
scheme justified by nebulous promises of an even better possible future.
Any attempt to achieve a quantum jump in the structure of the building
industry seemed to be doomed.

The many low and middle class purchasers of buildings were quite
unimpressed by the various proposals put forth. They couldn't have
cared less about detailed analyses of the reasons for failure or about
philosophical discussions of long term solutions. They suspected that the
intelligentsia was attempting to divert some of their economic gains (the
reduction in construction costs) in order to increase its own social power
and to enlarge its own empires (e.g. the training institutions and the
professional guild). The introduction of the new design technique had in
fact been followed by a noticeable shift in power from the upper
intellectual and professional classes to the middle and lower classes. The
latter, of course, did not want to see the former recoup their losses.

The attitude of the majority of the building purchasers was pragmatic
and their desires were quite simple: they wanted good designs for
buildings that would satisfy their needs and they wanted them *yesterday*.
All the political debate and the philosophical discussions of theoretical,
long-term solutions were only adding to the design delays and were
diverting attention from more promising short-term solutions to their
problems. The majority of the building purchasers had clearly defined

priorities: first, reduce the delays in producing the designs and then – only then – improve their quality. Although they did prefer professionally trained designers to "three week wonders", they preferred a "three week wonder" in three weeks to a professionally trained designer in three years. Increasing the rate of production of professional designers would not solve the crucial problem: the unnecessary delays in the process of designing buildings today.

The professionals countered these arguments by pointing out that the proliferation of unqualified practitioners was the underlying cause of both the time and the quality problems. A professional designer could not only prepare better plans, he could also prepare them somewhat faster than his less qualified colleagues. More importantly, the considerable time which the designers were forced to devote to supervising the elaborate testing procedures and to rework and corrections detracted greatly from their effective capacity.

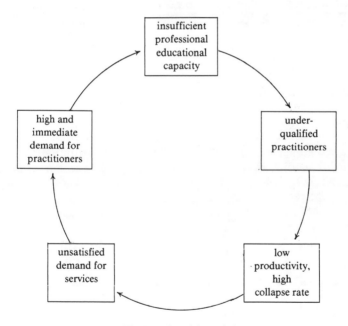

The Mocsian vicious circle

The professional designers also felt that the purchasers should concern themselves less with the time required to prepare building plans alone and direct their attention instead to the total time elapsed until the new building was standing and ready for use. By improving the quality of the designs, much time could be saved during the construction phase. In particular, the major delays caused by collapses and by the elaborate testing procedures could be all but eliminated. The issues of quality and time could not be separated as simply and neatly as the purchasers implicitly assumed. Until proper – i.e., professional – training facilities with adequate capacity existed, neither problem could be solved satisfactorily.

Such was the situation in the land of the Ret Up Moc (Glorious Society of Moc) when progress was interrupted by an epidemic (see also [Zinsser]*). The disease was highly contagious, moderately incapacitating but not lethal. Perhaps the respite in the hectic pace of Mocsian life would give time for much-needed reflection. Or was it just the calm before the storm?

---

* Square brackets [] enclose bibliographical references.

Chapter 1

Introduction

The story of the land of Moc is obviously pure fiction. Such a ridiculous story could never be true. Or could it?

It is the thesis of this book that the story of the land of Moc is true. "Only the names have been changed to protect the guilty." The time is not 2480 B.C. to 2400 B.C., but 1940 A.D. to the present. The industry is not an ancient construction industry, but our modern computer software industry. The location is not the cradle of civilization, but the industrialized part of the world. Within not so many years, the location may have grown to include essentially all populated areas of the planet Earth.

The true version of the story centers not on the designers of buildings, but on the programmers of our society's computers. (Throughout this book, the term "programmer" is used in its broadest sense and includes all persons directly involved in the detailed specification, design and development of computer software.) The products of these programmers' efforts are already of considerable – in some cases, even critical – importance to our society and to its various organizations and structures. Also of major consequence are the errors and shortcomings embedded in these products. The impact of both the positive and the negative aspects of these products on our life (both individual and collective) will certainly increase in the future. There will be no return to the softwareless, programmerless days of the recent past.

This book proposes that the activity of programming – specifying in

11

detail, designing and developing computer software – is by nature an engineering discipline but that it is not generally regarded as such in our society today. Some of the most serious consequences of our current non-engineering approach to programming are:
- disappointing and shoddy products, often containing simple errors of a fundamental nature,
- unnecessarily low productivity,
- frequent failures of such size that major projects must be aborted at a late stage of development,
- diversion of considerable effort to fundamentally unproductive tasks and
- generation of confusion, fear, frustration and misunderstanding among direct and indirect users of computer based systems.

Practitioners are illuded into believing that after a three week course, they are aware of just about all existing fundamental knowledge relevant to their endeavors; all that they then need to be fully effective is the right kit bag of small tools and a quickly attainable familiarity with the latest technical details in whatever specific area happens to be of current concern. The most unfortunate effect of this illusion is that it diverts into unrewarding directions their searches for ways to fundamentally improve the situation. Instead of taking the time to build a solid foundation for their current and future work, they are deceived into searching for a fountain of youth or a pot of gold at the end of the rainbow. They mistake technical details and minor facts of fleeting value for fundamental knowledge and understanding of lasting and general applicability. They mistake partial solutions to today's problems for complete solutions to yesterday's, today's and tomorrow's problems. The even more unfortunate ones are deluded into quixotic crusades.

Is programming an engineering discipline? What is an engineering discipline? In the narrowest sense, one can define engineering as those fields of activities which are concerned with applying the physical laws of matter and energy to the construction and operation of useful machines, buildings, bridges, etc. While this was certainly an adequate definition a century ago, it is too restrictive today. It seems to miss, for example, the essence of that part of electrical engineering concerned with electronics. While matter and energy are necessary aspects of the implementation of electronic devices and systems, the purely mathematical aspects of signal processing would seem to be of more fundamental importance. The abstract aspects of the various building blocks used by the electronics engineer and the manner in which he interconnects them to form a system with characteristics very different from those of its constituent parts seem somehow to be more essential than the physical embodiment of those elements and systems. (See note at the end of this chapter.)

The essential aspects of "engineering" would seem then to be not machines, matter and energy but rather the application of an extensive body of scientific knowledge (e.g. physics, chemistry, etc.) and logic (i.e., mathematics) to the task of designing and constructing something which takes on an identifiable, tangible form and which is of practical value. While this certainly does not capture all aspects of engineering work (in particular the creative and artistic aspects), it does seem to contain those key elements of engineering which differentiate it from other, non-engineering activities.

In deciding whether programming is, or is not, an engineering discipline one must, then, consider the following questions:
1. Does a significant body of scientific and mathematical knowledge exist which is relevant to programming?
2. Has the programmer mastered a substantial part of that body of knowledge?
3. Does the programmer actually make use of this knowledge in the course of performing his work?
4. Does the final result (software) take on an identifiable, tangible form?
5. Is the software produced of practical value?

Whether the body of knowledge relevant to programming is "significant" and whether a "substantial" part of it has been mastered by any particular programmer are, of course, subjective judgments. To make these judgments, it is useful to draw comparisons with other, accepted engineering fields. We can ask if the body of scientific and mathematical knowledge relevant to programming is similiar in character and size to that relevant to accepted engineering disciplines (for example as reflected in the technical literature). We can ask whether the formal education of a programmer is similar in quality and length to that of others whom we accept as engineers.

To answer the first question above, it is suggested that the reader peruse the professional literature in the field of computer science. Chapter 3 illustrates a small extract of this material. It is the contention of this book that the body of scientific and mathematical knowledge relevant to programming has become qualitatively and quantitatively comparable to that relevant to other engineering disciplines. Before 1960, this was probably not true. Around 1970, the point could be argued. Today, it is true.

In chapter 2 it is shown that – as in the case of the building designers in Moc in 2400 B.C. – only a small fraction of the programmers in our society today has successfully completed formal academic programs in computer science. While some others have acquired comparable knowledge in other ways, many practitioners have not mastered a substantial part of the relevant body of knowledge. Thus even if one does conclude that programming is an engineering discipline, not all programmers of today can be considered to be engineers.

The third question above should give rise to little controversy. Most programmers do regularly use in their work much of the relevant computer science knowledge they have. They may very well make use of a larger fraction of their store of professional knowledge in their daily work than engineers in other disiplines typically do.

The fourth question can also be answered affirmatively. A finished piece of software takes on several identifiable, tangible forms: printed listings, magnetic recordings, electronically stored patterns, video displays as well as various types of documents intended for human readers. The behaviour exhibited by a software system (or more precisely, by a computer executing the software) can be observed, tested and measured.

While not all software, after it has been produced, has any practical value, much of it must be of considerable practical value – otherwise we would not expend ever increasing amounts of effort to produce more and more. Almost all, if not all, software produced or attempted was at least originally intended to have practical value, that is, to satisfy some real need. Even the recent wave of game software for microcomputer systems must be recognized as satisfying a demand for entertainment and therefore as having practical value. Much of it certainly has economic value.

A few writers and professional groups do seem to have recognized programming as an engineering discipline. Norbert Wiener described programming (he used the term "taping") as "a highly skilled task for a professional man of a very specialized type" [Wiener, p. 156]. The term "software engineering" was used, albeit more in a provocative than in a descriptive manner, as early as 1968, when the NATO Science Committee sponsored a conference in Europe on that subject. The term "software engineering" was chosen as the title of the conference in order to express "the need for software manufacture to be based on the types of theoretical foundations and practical disciplines that are traditional in the established branches of engineering" [Naur and Randell, p. 13]. Since 1975, the Institute of Electrical and Electronics Engineers in the U.S.A. has been publishing a scientific journal entitled "Transactions on Software Engineering". Also since the mid-1970's, several professional societies have sponsored various conferences and symposia with titles including the term "software engineering". The Association for Computing Machinery has founded a Special Interest Group on Software Engineering (SIGSOFT). In 1979, Richard E. Fairley, the chairman of the IEEE Computer Society's Subcommittee on Software Engineering Education, stated that "software engineering has evolved into a major subdiscipline of computer science and engineering. Although much remains to be done, a body of knowledge and a set of guidelines have emerged which incorporate traditional engineering values into the production and maintenance of software systems." [Fairley]

While a definite trend toward the recognition of programming as an engineering discipline can be discerned in the professional, technical and trade literature, this trend is not a particularly strong one. Such recognition has not yet become widespread by any means [Kimm, p. 5]. Programming is probably more widely recognized as an engineering discipline in academic computer science circles and among graduates of college level computer science programs than anywhere else. Such recognition is probably less pronounced among software houses and other software producers. Most purchasers and users of software products would undoubtedly respond to the suggestion that programming is an engineering discipline with an unbelieving smile, if not a cynical laugh. While they might wish that this were the case, and might feel that it should be the case, few, if any, would agree that it is the case today. But probably only relatively few people connected with the software industry have ever really given the matter any serious thought at all.

The programmers of our software industry work in many places in our economy. They can be found within the various organizations which directly utilize their products. These programmers are most frequently grouped together in the EDP department, information systems department, etc., as it is variously called, but some can already be found directly in the user departments. Most employees of software houses, many employees of systems houses and some members of consulting organizations are programmers in our sense of the word. Quite a few programmers do not belong to any organization, but work as free lance systems analysts or coders (programmers in the narrow sense of the term) or as independent consultants of various types. Considerable numbers of programmers can, of course, be found in the software divisions of computer manufacturers. Finally, programmers are at work in growing numbers in organizations which develop products containing computers (especially microprocessors) as an integral component. In short, they are scattered over many places. In the future, they may very well become even more widely spread throughout society and its organizations.

There are many aspects of the social responsibilities associated with the programming of our computers (or with the application of any important technology, for that matter). It is convenient and useful to divide these aspects into two broad categories. The first category deals with *what* computers should (and/or can) be programmed to do and with the social consequences of *what* they do or may be made to do. The second category deals with *how* they are programmed to do what we have decided they should be set to do and with the social consequences of *how* we program them.

The *what* issues include, for example, such questions as the following:

Should the accounts of company X be processed by computer? Its payroll?

Should typesetting be computerized?

Should credit information on individuals be stored in computer systems?

Should such credit information be exchanged automatically between computers in different companies? What legal rights might be infringed by such exchange?

What restrictions should be placed generally on the computer storage and exchange of personal data?

Which aspects of controlling nuclear reactors should be performed by computer instead of by a human operator?

Which aspects of controlling commercial air traffic should be computerized?

Which functions of a country's military defense systems should be performed by computer systems? Of its offensive systems?

What safety precautions against computer failure should be included in such systems?

Which, if any, of the tasks currently performed by factory workers on production line X in company Y should be performed by computer controlled machines instead?

What are the meaningful and proper roles of a computer in the home? Of a "personal" computer in the office?

Should we set out to design a computer controlled robot for the home which will vacuum the floors and dust the furniture by itself (without damaging delicate antique glassware on the shelves) – thus enabling a considerable number of people to devote much effort to other tasks which also need to be performed?

Should the main catalog of a national library be stored on an on-line computer system and be accessible by all private citizens from their homes?

Should the full texts of the publications in that library be similarly stored and made available within seconds to remotely located users?

What benefits would thereby accrue to the user? to society as a whole? How can the rights of copyright holders be adequately protected? Should the full texts of all publications or only of those that are out of print be made so available?

Should the contents of newspapers, magazines and books be distributed via computerized data transmission networks instead of in printed form?

Should we attempt to employ computer systems to diagnose diseases and other medical conditions (partially replacing the physician)?

Should we attempt to employ computer systems to prescribe therapy (replacing the physician to an even greater extent)?

Should company X install a computerized electronic mail and teleconferencing system, enabling its employees to work at home three days per week?

The answers chosen to questions of this type obviously have major short, medium and long-term consequences for many members of society. The list of such issues could, of course, be continued almost indefinitely.

The *how* issues include not only questions of technical method which are of direct concern only to the programmer, but also – and more importantly for our purpose – questions of consequence to other members of society. While many of these consequences are indirect (involving the effects of software quality, the availability of new products and services, the education of a new, potentially large group of professionals, etc.), they are often more significant than one might at first expect. Examples of such *how* issues include:

Should we entrust programming to professionally trained specialists, to less thoroughly trained technicians, to persons of other specialities who have been briefly familiarized with programming or to some combination of the three?

If to some combination, what is the best balance between the several types of programmers?

What formal and informal programs for the original training of the several types of programmers should be instituted?

What training capacity is needed? Who should conduct the training?

How are programmers to be kept informed of new techniques, methods, discoveries and other developments of value to them in their work? How do we encourage them to keep themselves informed and up to date?

How do we ensure that programmers have convenient access to and maintain an adequate awareness of the available bodies of knowledge relevant to their work? How do we ensure that they take full advantage thereof?

What balance should be established between the numbers of programmers who are

– employees of the department using their products,

- employees of a special department or staff of the same organization,
- employees of other organizations producing and supplying software and related services and
- independent professionals?

What balance should be established among the various areas of specialization in the programming field, e.g.

- application software (financial systems, inventory control systems, production planning and control systems, order processing systems, etc.),
- system software (compilers, operating systems, data base management systems, data communications, etc.),
- management,
- teaching,
- research, etc.?

In which areas should we attempt to increase our capabilities (e.g. translation between natural languages, pattern recognition, voice output, speech recognition, robot control, graphics, storing and processing pictorial data, supporting high level decision making, etc.)?

What formal standards for the professional and/or technical qualifications required of programmers should be established (if any)? Who should set and enforce them?

Which programming activities should be performed only by persons possessing such formal qualifications?

What are the social and economic consequences of not setting or not enforcing standards for programmers' qualifications? Is it necessary to set such standards? Can society afford not to set them?

To what extent is the public exposed to the risk of possible injury or economic loss resulting from the malfunction of computer systems (hardware or software)? How severe is the potential damage? How can the associated risk be minimized?

What precautions can and should be taken to ascertain that the software in any particular system is free of faults that could cause catastrophic failure?

To what extent should the general public be educated in subjects related to programming? Should, for example, every school child be required to take a course in computer appreciation and/or computer programming?

The *what* issues are, perhaps, of greater fundamental importance in the long run than the *how* issues. But our shortfall in achieving what we have set out to do with computers and in achieving what we know to be possible to do with them is so great that the *how* issues appear to be, at least now and in the near future, of greater consequence to society. As long as the large gap continues to exist between what is possible and what we set out to do on the one hand and what we can, in practice, reliably achieve on the other hand, many of the *what* questions are academic. Primarily for this reason, this book deals only with *how* issues.

That is not to say that we should not concern ourselves with the *what* issues. In fact they have received attention in important works, for example [Wiener] (1950), [Dreyfus] (1972) and [Weizenbaum] (1976), just to cite a few. They will undoubtedly receive more attention in the future, and that is certainly justified.

Many of those deeply concerned with the *what* issues point out that mankind should not try to do everything which is technologically possible to do. This is undoubtedly true. This proposition seems, however, to be interpreted by some to mean or to imply that we should limit attempts to extend our technological capability. On the contrary, the two propositions

1. mankind should strive to achieve the technological capability to do whatever he decides he should do and
2. mankind should not do everything which his technological capability enables him to do

contrast with one another, but they are not contradictory. In fact, attempting to maximize mankind's social and economic welfare necessitates that he 1) strive to increase his capability to do all kinds of things and 2) exercise the good judgment and will power to apply this capability in ways which contribute to his well being and to refrain from applying it in ways which would detract from his well being. The *how* issues referred to above relate to the first of these two propositions; the *what* issues arise from the conflicts inherent in the decision-making processes implied by the second.

The application of the first proposition above to programming places a responsibility on programmers to strive to improve their abilities to create software which does what has been specified and which does not do anything else which would cause injury, loss or inconvenience to society in general or to its individual members. In particular, this places certain obligations on programmers with respect to the quality and correctness of their products and especially with respect to their ability to verify that correctness. In chapter 2, it is shown that we are very far from fulfilling this responsibility – despite the fact that methods are known which, when used appropriately and skillfully, enable programmers to improve the quality of their products very considerably. Some of these methods appear in chapter 3.

The application of the first proposition above to programming also places a responsibility on programmers to strive to improve their productivity. While productivity does not affect what one can in *principle* do with a given technology, it does affect, often very fundamentally, what society can in *practice* do with it.

As mentioned earlier, this book is concerned with *how* issues only. These issues are of immediate importance and concern but are currently receiving much less attention than they properly deserve. Our inadequate resolution of them is currently impeding our progress in applying computer systems to many tasks that are both possible and socially desirable.

Programmers, both collectively and individually, have a social responsibility to improve their capabilities very considerably and more rapidly than they are now doing. Other members of society have an obligation to help, guide and, if necessary, coerce programmers to fulfill this responsibility better in the future. These responsibilities and obligations have been overlooked too long. The social costs of continuing to overlook them are increasing rapidly and will soon become unacceptably high.

This book is directed primarily to the following groups, who will – actively or passively – influence strongly our software future:

– software practitioners (today's "system analysts" and "programmers"),
– managers of software development groups,
– educators (both in academia and in secondary schools),
– software users and user management and
– persons responsible for the formulation of public and private policy in the above areas.

This book, it is hoped, will contribute to an increased awareness of our present and probable future problems in the areas of software design, development and application and will stimulate discussion of the pertinent issues by all parties concerned. While it ends with general suggestions for actions to be taken by each of the groups listed above, it is beyond its scope to attempt to develop a final, detailed action plan for every party involved in shaping our software future. That effort requires the active participation of members of all of the above mentioned groups.

Note. The pronoun "he" is used in this book strictly in the sense of the second definition given on page 1041 of "Webster's Third New International Dictionary of the English Language Unabridged", published by G.&C. Merriam Company. Springfield, Massachusetts, U.S.A., 1976. I.e., no connotation of gender is to be attributed to this pronoun or to any of its several declined forms as they appear in this book.

Chapter 2

The practice of software design and development: yesterday and today

What is not fully understood is not possessed.

Johann Wolfgang Goethe (1749–1832)

Ignorance gives a sort of eternity to prejudice, and perpetuity to error.

Robert Hall (1764–1831)

The practice of software design and development yesterday and today has many parallels in the practice of civil engineering in the land of Moc between 2480 and 2400 B.C. The practice of software design and development has been, and still is, characterized by a similarly high rate of Mocsian-like "collapses". Whereas in Moc buildings collapsed only during construction, our software systems "collapse" not only during construction but also *after* they have been put into service. Design and construction by trial and error (following the Mocsian motto "try building it and see if it collapses") seems to be a widely used and accepted approach to the task of software development.

Every engineering discipline has its collapses, of course. Collapses occur much more frequently in the area of software development, however, than they do in any other field of engineering. The collapse of a bridge or building during construction is a newsworthy event; the public is surprised – precisely because such events are seldom. The discovery of a design error of comparable consequence in commercial aircraft in service, to cite another example, is a similarly unusual and surprising event. Such failures usually make headlines, lead to changes in the practice of the corresponding field of engineering and become key examples in engineering education. When these errors are discovered, the perpetrator is expected, and normally legally obliged, to make amends. Major collapses are so frequent in the software field, however, that only the very largest and most spectacular ones are considered newsworthy; most receive relatively little attention. They come as disappointments, certainly, but not as surprises. They are accepted as the norm that they have come to be, occurring so frequently that it would be unrealistic to expect the perpetrator to make amends.

In every engineering discipline, trial and error also has its place, but only when the designer is knowingly and intentionally working in new areas, "pushing the state of the art" as it is sometimes called. In such cases, the "trial and error" approach normally takes the form of scientific experimentation. Experiments are designed to yield answers to the open questions, to discriminate between alternative hypotheses, to extend the limiting frontiers of knowledge. The risks are consciously accepted and appropriate precautions are taken. Trial and error is not acceptable when the designer is working in areas in which his own personal expertise is lacking and is not up to the "state of the art". In such a case, the engineer is expected to familiarize himself with the relevant literature and accumulated experience of others before embarking into what is, for him, new territory. To do otherwise is considered irresponsible.

This attitude does not seem to be the norm now in the field of software development. Experiments designed to yield specific information needed by the designer are not commonplace. All too often, the software developer makes use of the "trial and error" approach in its crudest form instead of consulting the often rich and voluminous professional literature. In many cases, this is understandable: The programmer is often unaware of the limitations in his knowledge and experience until an unexpected collapse occurs. Many practicing programmers today are unable to read the computer science literature. Often they are even unaware of its very existence. The other literature which they can understand often contains insufficient detail, contains exaggerated claims, is inadequately indexed and/or is not easily and quickly accessible.

The reasons for this state of affairs also have their parallels in the state of affairs in Mocsian civil engineering in 2400 B.C. Our programmers – like the Mocsian designers – have had little opportunity and even less incentive to attend professional training programs. Our educational systems have not responded adequately to the rapid development of the field of software engineering. The economic pressures of the market place seem to value a "three week wonder" in three weeks at least as highly as a professionally trained practitioner in a few years. In any event, there are not enough of either to satisfy the rapidly growing demand. The short-term problems are so great that we concentrate on them, knowingly postponing attention to the mid- and long-term problems – even when we recognize that the latter may turn out to have even more severe consequences.

The following randomly selected anecdotes and short narratives illustrate the problematic state of affairs in the field of software development. All these stories are true; only unimportant details have been modified in some cases to preserve anonymity. While they do not give a complete, statistically balanced picture of the software industry yesterday or today (the success stories are underrepresented), these narratives are – unfortunately – typical of the goings-on in this field.

The evolution of the nature of software projects is reflected in these stories. In the 1950's, even advanced software "systems" tended to be limited in scope and interacted little, if at all, with other systems. In the 1960's, the typical software system was larger in scope, represented a more ambitious undertaking and, especially in the latter part of the decade, interacted closely with several other systems. "Integrated" systems received much attention and became something of an ideal for planners and designers until a number of spectacular collapses at the end of the 1960's and in the early 1970's had a sobering effect. The 1970's constituted a period of somewhat steadier (but still rapid) growth and a sort of consolidation. While larger, ambitious software projects continued to be developed, time sharing systems and the advent of the minicomputer led to a renewed popularity of smaller applications which exhibited at most only loose interaction with other systems. With the appearance of the microcomputers in the late 1970's, this trend continued, supported by disillusionment and disappointment with the software industry's inabililty to satisfy the demand for larger systems running on "mainframe" (i.e. relatively large) computers.

When reading the following narratives, the reader should note how the same problems and causes recur over and over again in many different contexts. We do not seem to be learning from our mistakes. While the errors being committed are much the same over the decades, their negative consequences are becoming ever more serious as the systems being developed become larger and more complex.

While it is obvious that the software industry has increased its capacity – in terms of both total output and individual project size – tremendously over the last 20 to 30 years, the following narratives raise a question regarding the improvement of software quality. Some observers feel that the quality of the typical software product has actually declined over this period. Others feel that it declined during the 1960's, reached a low in the early 1970's, and has been slowly improving since then. In any event, it is clear that software quality has been a major problem for more than two decades and still leaves much to be desired. And, also just as in Moc, the problem of insufficient capacity is still with us.

The 1950's

Computer programming for graduate students only?

For several years in the 1950's, a single course in computer programming was offered at a particular engineering school. Considered to be a very specialized course, it was offered only to graduate students. The professor in charge of the course was somewhat taken aback one day when a sophomore applied to enroll in the course. The student wanted to take a professional elective but lacked the prerequisites for other courses in which he was interested. He was admitted to the course and completed it successfully.

Thus, a significant gap between supply and demand for software oriented education was filled satisfactorily – perhaps for the last time?

Computer programming for freshmen, too

Two years later, this course as well as other, new ones in computer programming had become so popular among undergraduates that it was decided to offer a freshman elective in computing. A high level of interest was expected; some predicted that as many as 10% of the freshman class might be interested in the course. The first meeting was a chaos – well over 20% of the freshman class tried to enroll. The number of instructors available was hopelessly insufficient to meet the demand.

It was assumed, of course, that this large gap between supply and demand for the education of programmers was only a transient phenomenon. Little did one know.

Programming in machine language

For a popular computer model, no assembler or compiler was available. All programming was done in machine language. A few programs were available from the user's group. One of these was an interpreter which effectively extended the machine's instruction set to include floating point arithmetical operations, trigonometric functions, etc. This interpreter seemed to be robust and was successfully used by several installations. The documentation for the interpreter was brief, unpolished in appearance but generally adequate.

Retrogressive plagiarism

A relatively sophisticated assembler was written for a medium sized computer system. An extensive library of macroinstructions was provided with this assembler, including in-line routines and subroutines for magnetic tape operations, error handling, searching and manipulating tables, calculating various mathematical functions, etc. A few years later, essentially the same assembly system was made available for a newer, more popular computer. For the new machine, however, only an extremely meager library of essentially useless routines was provided. Especially disappointing was the complete lack of library routines for tape operations.

This step backward went unnoticed by many persons involved with the new machine.

The inefficient assembler

The algorithm used for searching the library in an otherwise well-designed assembler system was very inefficient. A simple modification would have more than doubled the average speed of the searching operation.

Apparently, the system's designers lacked the time, the ability or the inclination to analyze and compare systematically the execution time required by several alternative searching algorithms.

A software tool for hardware designers

Within a computer manufacturer's engineering organization, a software system was developed which provided extensive support to a hardware design group. The system checked that hardware designs fulfilled certain technical criteria, contained complete and consistent information, etc. It also prepared printed logic diagrams in final form. It contained a program generator for creating checking routines for newly defined circuits. It produced useful results for some time, although some parts of the system had a cumbersome structure and required continual revision.

Many homework assignments = a system?

A software system for analyzing electrical circuits was prepared by an engineer who taught an evening course in computing to student engineers. Some of the homework assignments consisted of writing certain routines for the system. As a result, the various parts of the system were quite heterogeneous, especially with respect to their quality and the distribution of errors.

Later, instructors and students of this and comparable courses wondered if this was a good way of developing a software system and if this was a good way of training new programmers.

The disappearing programs

To facilitate running students' programs, many university computing centers installed a monitor, a primitive form of what we would today call an operating system. Many a student received back not only his output listing, but also that of the student whose program was placed after his own in the run queue. The second student, of course, received no listing at all. This problem was caused by minor mistakes in the first or last card in the deck of cards submitted by the student. Because many of the students were inexperienced, such errors occurred moderately frequently.

Few seemed concerned that neophyte programmers were forced to suffer the consequences of errors and oversights for which others (the system's designers) were responsible. On the other hand, perhaps this was a good way to introduce the neophytes to the realities of the software world.

The 1960's

Fully tried and tested?

A FORTRAN compiler was supplied with a new computer system installed in a small, new computer center in the early 1960's. Purportedly, the compiler had been tested by the computer manufacturer's software department and had already been successfully installed at other customers' sites. When users at the computer center were unable to compile even the simplest program, the manufacturer's software support representatives were called in. After many hours, they identified an error in the compiler and applied a temporary modification. Some time later, the error was permanently corrected in a revised version of the compiler.

Such problems were attributed to the newness of the industry, of the techniques for software development and distribution and of the machine. In the future, difficulties of this type would constitute the exception rather than the rule – or would they?

The impossible error message

Personnel in a computing center noticed that if a particular program was assembled with a certain tape in a particular tape drive, an error message something like "ERROR NUMBER 982 IN PASS 4 PHASE 2" was printed out. The normal documentation did not list this error code. A special document, intended only for the computer manufacturer's own software staff, explained the error roughly as follows: "An internal system error has been detected. This error message should never occur."

Because the error message did not appear when other tapes were mounted in the drive in question, an error in a tape error routine in or before the cited pass and phase was suspected. An examination of some of the corresponding programs in the assembly system revealed that each contained several different tape error routines. It appeared that the various tape error routines contained several errors of different types.

One can only wonder why the system's designers had, apparently, never heard of subroutines (a program element already well known by that time) and had never thought about "user friendliness".

It works – most of the time.

In the same installation, a standard program for sorting data on tape was used. Most executions of the sort program were successful. Occasionally, however, extra data records would suddenly appear during a merging phase. Again, an error in a tape error routine was suspected.

If you can't fix the errors, ignore them.

During the development of a large software system, a software house was severely hampered by a very high rate of tape errors occurring on the customer's computer system. In order to enable compilations to run to completion, the software house removed from the compiler all tests for tape errors. This permitted the software house to proceed with program development, but the compiled programs behaved erratically when the customer tested them.

While the approach taken would seem to have been a practical one in a certain sense, one must question whether it was a responsible one. In all likelihood, its perpetrators did not weigh fairly the cost to others of the consequences of their decision.

Cards, cards, everywhere

A moderately large software system was supplied to an important customer by a well-known software house. Preparing the data for this system each month ("loading the data base") was a cumbersome operation. First, a deck of some 25,000 cards was reproduced. The two decks were then sorted using an electromechanical card sorter. Each deck was sorted into a different, complicated sequence (ascending on some fields, descending on others, mixed on still others) necessitating approximately 15 passes through the sorter. Three to six shifts of two or three people each were required to perform the entire operation. The sorted decks were then read and processed by a series of computer programs which copied the data onto magnetic tape in the format required by the software system. The operation of this set of programs was also intricate and problematic. The sequence check built into the program usually detected sequence errors, of course.

A newly arrived programmer, who was totally confused by his first confrontation with so many piles of so many cards in various intermediate stages of sorting, scattered all over the tab room, was frightened by the possibility that he might be asked to supervise this operation some day. In about a week, he designed and wrote a program system which used a standard tape sorting program to do all sorting. His system, which "loaded the data base" in a few hours, required an absolute minimum of manual intervention.

After the improved system was successfully implemented, its creator learned that software "experts" had earlier gone on record as saying that it was impossible to use the standard sort program for this application.

This raises some doubt regarding the adequacy of the education and training of these – and other – software "experts".

The TOP SECRET blank pages

In a particular department of one country's defense establishment, a series of programs printed a long classified report. The security legend was printed at the top and at the bottom of each page. In addition, each page was numbered. Because of logical flaws in the programs' printing routines, a few pages would, from time to time, be printed which contained one or both security legends but no data. They could not be deleted from the report without introducing a discrepancy in the page count. This led to the ludicrous situation in which blank pages were classified "TOP SECRET" and registered accordingly.

A shell game

A library of mathematical subroutines contained four different subroutines for numerically solving differential equations. All four were tried in an attempt to find the solution to a particular equation. One subroutine terminated abnormally with an overflow error. The other three yielded significantly different answers. The documentation was incomplete and of no help in determining which, if any, of the routines gave the correct answer to the problem at hand.

It is sobering to ponder what the consequences of applying an incorrect solution to the real problem at hand might have been.

Error messages simplified to the extreme?

For one of its computer series, an important computer manufacturer supplied a compiler which issued only one error message stating that an error had been found in the source program. Neither the type of error nor the source statement in error was identified.

Again, a system's users were forced to pay the price of the designer's convenience – or was it his laziness or inability?

Send it to the field – working or not.

To facilitate the sales of a new computer, a program which simulated an older, popular computer built by a competitor was developed. The simulator was not completed on time. Because some sales offices had already arranged customer demonstrations, a preliminary version of the simulator was made available to the manufacturer's field organization. Rigged demonstrations were partially successful, but all attempts to demonstrate the simulator with customers' programs failed to produce satisfactory results. In a few cases, use of the simulator even caused an otherwise extremely rare I/O fault condition to arise. Action by the repair personnel was required to reset the condition and to restore the system to an operational state. The simulator was revised several times before it became reliable.

A few wondered silently whether the rigged demonstrations constituted deception of an almost criminal degree.

Can software failure bankrupt a company?

A major computer manufacturer installed several very large, fast computers in a new model series. When it was discovered that both the hardware and the operating system were unreliable, failing randomly but frequently, many customers withheld payment of the monthly rental fees. The manufacturer soon resolved the hardware problems, but the operating system – despite many corrections and revisions – continued to function unsatisfactorily. The manufacturer's cash flow situation became very strained; some observers of the industry expected the company to become insolvent. Finally, large infusions of loan capital enabled the supplier to remain in business while the errors in the operating system were being corrected.

Insecure data

Appended to the output listing given to a customer by a computing center was an extract of the computing center's own payroll. It turned out that the customer's program had not run successfully. As a result, it did not write an end of file marker on his output tape, which had previously been used for a payroll calculation. When a job control statement in the customer's card deck called for his output tape to be printed, the latter part of the payroll file was also printed out.

Theory simplifies practice.

In a large information system, data relating to individual persons was indexed by the person's name. A method was required for locating data on a particular person even when the name available to the searcher was misspelled. This was to be accomplished by transforming the available name into a kind of abbreviation in such a way that 1) typical misspellings of a name transformed to the same abbreviation as the correct name and 2) as few as possible different correct names transformed to the same abbreviation.

The data processing department had obtained several different suggested rules for transforming the names into abbreviations. One rule had been programmed and tested using a large collection of representative names. The program contained very intricate logic and had a very confused structure. Some suspected that it contained errors.

A new programmer was given the task of identifying and correcting any errors in the existing transformation program, programming the other transformation rules and evaluating the several different rules. After about two months, he had managed to find and correct a few errors in the program but had otherwise made disappointingly little progress. When he estimated that some two months would be required to program each of the remaining transformation rules but could not predict when the project would be finished, his manager asked a consultant for advice.

The consultant observed that such a transformation of names was homomorphic to (and could therefore be represented by) a finite automaton with a small number of states. The table defining the automaton's state transitions and outputs could be derived in a more or less straightforward manner from the given transformation rules. One program could be written which, given any table of state transitions and outputs, would perform the corresponding name transformation. The table-driven program would be much simpler in structure than the one already written and could be used without modification for all of the several transformation rules to be evaluated. It was decided to use this approach.

In attempting to formulate the state transition table for the first rule for transforming names, it was quickly discovered that the specified rule was ambiguous and contained inconsistencies. This situation had apparently led the original programmer to become confused, without his realizing the true underlying reason. His attempts to correct specific errors as he discovered them resulted unavoidably in the introduction of other errors. The many iterations of this trial and error approach to getting his program right led ultimately to the unsystematic structure of his program. His approach would never have led to success, of course, for he had been – unknowingly – trying to program an unprogrammable process.

The transformation rule was modified in a way that appeared linguistically reasonable to obtain an unambiguous and consistent rule. In two to three months, the proposed new program for transforming names was written, the state transition tables for the several rules were formulated and the analysis and comparison of all transformation rules were completed. Using the original approach, it would have taken much longer to complete the project – assuming that the attempt would have been successful at all.

After his first discussion with the consultant, the programmer, who had had no previous computer science training, obtained from a library and read several moderately sophisticated articles on finite automata and closely related subjects. During the course of the project, he became something of an expert in applying his newly acquired knowledge to practical problems.

The 1970's

An integrated collapse in the new world

One company had decided in the mid-1960's to implement a truly integrated information system to satisfy both operational and manage-

ment needs. The design specified subsystems for order entry and processing, sales forecasting, inventory control of finished goods, finance and
accounting, market research, product design and development, production planning and scheduling, materials planning, personnel, management reporting, budgeting, etc. The various subsystems were to be
implemented over a period of about 7 years. The system would be based
on a very large and expensive multi-computer configuration at the central
site with a data communications network linking the company's various
offices. A large number of sophisticated video and printing terminals
would be located at the many users' locations.

The main goals of this system were to provide more complete, accurate
and timely information for management decision making, to optimize
operational control (e.g. to optimize production schedules, inventories,
etc.) and to increase the efficiency of clerical and other operations.

Unfortunately, these noble goals were never realized. In the early
1970's, shortly before the system was to be completed, it became pain-
fully obvious to all concerned that the system could not be developed and
implemented. It was finally recognized that the plan was too ambitious
and that it was based on overly optimistic and unrealistic assumptions.
The project culminated in a meeting of top management which was
subdued in form but explosive in content and impact. The net result was
that the project was abandoned. Many key members of management
both within and outside the information systems area left the employ of
the company, some voluntarily, some not. The estimated net loss exceeded $10 million.

Following this unpleasant experience, the pendulum of data processing
policy swung to the opposite extreme in this company. For many years,
an overly conservative approach toward EDP was followed by management, who were determined to avoid the risk of such a catastrophe
occurring again. Many potentially profitable medium sized EDP systems
were never seriously considered. The opportunity cost associated with
this policy was never estimated but was undoubtedly substantial.

In the design and development of this integrated system, errors similar
to those made in situations described earlier were committed. But here
they were made in a system of much greater scope and involving many
more people—developers and users alike. The consequences of the
system's shortcomings were no longer of an annoying but acceptable
nature (as, for example, in the stories "It works—most of the time" and

"Cards, cards, everywhere" on page 30). In this case, the consequences of the system's shortcomings had such widespread repercussions that its users could not accept it. The unfortunate result of this major failure was an overly conservative reaction which would later be observed again in other companies.

An integrated collapse in the old world

It was generally fashionable in the 1960's to point out that the old world was some years behind the new in matters concerning EDP. Unfortunately, however, the old world's programmers of our computers did *not* lag behind their brethren on the other side of the Atlantic when it came to creating spectacular collapses.

The management of a medium sized industrial company approved in the mid-1960's a plan to design and implement an integrated information system. The system was to become operational at the end of the decade. The project was clearly showing signs of great strain at the turn of the decade; the collapse came shortly thereafter.

It was intended that this system should contribute to the profitability of the company, support the management decision making process by providing appropriate information, projections and proposed decisions and that it should relieve people of routine, operational tasks. Subsystems were foreseen for sales forecasting, order processing, production planning and scheduling, materials management, personnel, finance and accounting, planning and budgeting, management control, etc. Each subsystem was further subdivided into groups of closely related business functions and finally into individual programs.

This system was based on a centralized computer system with several subsidiary computer centers at key office and plant locations. A data communications network was planned to link the various computers and users' terminals.

Several hundred man years of effort were invested in the specification, design, development and implementation of the application software. When the collapse came, quite a number of programs were running, a few of them well, but the functions and services provided to the system's users were somehow not quite what they wanted and had expected. Just why this situation came about never really became completely clear, but ineffective communication between management, the system's intended users and the development team appeared to have been an important part of the cause.

In the early 1970's, management decided to abandon the project. Only a small fraction of the results of the project could be meaningfully salvaged. The EDP manager, the project manager, several key members of the project team and certain members of the company's top management team were replaced.

Considering these independent integrated collapses in the new and old worlds (see above) in the light of Murphy's Law ("if anything can go wrong, it will"), one might expect a single integrated collapse in both worlds to occur sometime in the future.

The $1,000 loop

In the early 1970's, a sophisticated simulation system for a particular class of business problems was designed and developed by a consulting organization. It was used successfully both for consulting projects and as a teaching tool in seminars. During its long, useful life, its users (the consultants) were plagued by the many errors it contained. The most expensive of these "bugs" was an infinite loop in one subroutine; this loop once consumed about $1,000 worth of computer time on a very large and fast time sharing system before the consultants interrupted the run. In the early years of its use, most errors discovered were in those parts of the programs which simulated unusual business strategies. Many years later, when the system was translated to another higher level language, a series of errors were discovered which gave rise to the possibility of division by zero. The original version of the program contained a control statement which caused run-time error messages to be suppressed (including error messages indicating division by zero).

The consequences of the errors in this relatively limited system were correspondingly limited and thus acceptable. More seriously, many of the users of this system experienced here, for the first time, the possibilities and potential dangers of computer based systems. Given the difficulties they encountered, it would not be surprising if they were to become rather skeptical potential users of future computer systems.

Fully tried and tested? (2)

A business firm designed and implemented a software system for sales forecasting. The plans for this system called for several standard programs available from the hardware manufacturer to be incorporated into the new forecasting system. During the implementation phase, several major errors were discovered in these programs, which had purportedly been successfully implemented in several other companies. One error, found by a consultant to the user, was caused by a fundamental mistake in the mathematical analysis underlying the formulae imbedded in the program. Other errors were simple "bugs". The computer manufacturer's representatives could not explain why the errors had not been detected by previous users. A new program, specified by the consultant and written by the user's programming staff, replaced the manufacturer's erroneous programs.

Cases of "fully tried and tested" software found to be unusable were by this time no longer surprising. They were fairly common throughout the 1960's (see page 29). The earlier assumption that they represented a transient phenomenon was beginning to be proved false.

Sometimes software systems do work—but not by chance.

One of the purposes of the sales forecasting system outlined above was to provide data needed by an inventory control system being developed. The development team consisted of representatives from the company's management, the inventory control department, other departments directly affected by the new system and the EDP department as well as several consultants. Of the many issues that had to be resolved in the course of this project, two are of particular interest here.

A set of formulae had been specially derived for the system which could be solved only by iterative approximation. One of the members of the team was concerned that the iterative method might not always converge, that it might sometimes converge to an undesired solution or that problems of numerical accuracy might arise. A lengthy mathematical analysis showed that no such problems would arise in the particular case at hand, but that a particular kind of non-linear interpolation in a table was required in one part of the computation.

Another member of the team was concerned about the possible

consequences of the unavoidable delays in the man-machine communication in this batch system. The system would issue recommended replenishment orders for action by the inventory control department. The possibly modified orders would then be entered into this and other computer based systems by the responsible persons. It was, in principle, possible that before the person had acted upon one recommendation, the system could issue another related recommendation. Analysis showed that the tentative design would in some situations indeed lead to considerable and serious mutual confusion between the man and the machine.

Such a possibility was, of course, unacceptable to the user department. The system's designers decided to define a number of states of recommended orders. For each state, they specified which events would cause the system to generate which messages and recommendations and which state transitions would occur. A number of discussions between the designers and the users were required to define the states, the transitions between them and the behaviour of the system in all combinations of states and events. During these discussions, a number of possible sequences of events came to light which no one had considered before and which forced the user to think through in detail what he really wanted from the system.

The system was implemented successfully and employed profitably for many years.

If one examines the narratives of the more successful systems and computer projects, a symbiosis of theoretical and practical capabilities is often observed (see e.g. "Theory simplifies practice", page 33). In the less successful situations, one of these two important ingredients tends to be lacking (e.g. in the following narrative).

A data base: a good foundation?

A company decided to implement a large and ambitious information system for production and inventory control. The development plan called first for a major part of the necessary data base to be developed. Then the other, operational parts of the system were to be designed and developed. After several years of hard work, a data base had been established (at considerable cost). Because the operational parts of the system had not yet been designed or implemented, there was little incentive to take the time and to expend the effort necessary to keep the data base up to date. Because it was not maintained, the one or two occasional applications which did use it could not be meaningfully executed. Therefore, they also fell into disuse. In the meantime, it became evident that organizational changes should be introduced in the factories before implementing the operational production and inventory control applications, but no specific action was ever taken on these organizational issues.

The net result of the project was that after several years, a considerable investment had been made in an obsolete, seldom used data base. Perhaps equally important, valuable resources were diverted from the development of other, potentially profitable information systems in this company.

Reasonably careful attention was paid here to the technicalities of data base systems. Unfortunately, too little attention was given to the system's practical utilization. Because of this unrealistic, imbalanced approach, the system was technically successful but commercially a failure, making no significant net contribution to the company which developed and implemented it.

Data base management systems: panacea, placebo or poison?

The management of a large company approved a proposal for a large EDP system for order entry and processing. The company sold their products through a large number of sales offices and distributors. Each day, many small orders were processed and delivered. Because the locations of the delivery warehouses did not coincide with the locations of the sales offices, the new system would include a nationwide data communications network connecting the various sales offices and warehouses with the very large data base at the national data processing center.

Detailed studies were made of the requirements the system would have to fulfill, the data volumes, etc. An extensive investigation of several available and planned data base systems was made. Finally, the hardware and software supplier was selected and the development of the application software was initiated.

From the outset, some members of the project team were concerned about the system's response time. A special group of technical experts from the supplier's organization analyzed this potential problem area and concluded that while no precise forecasts of the response time could be made, serious problems were not to be expected.

The system was developed and installed and the implementation phase began. As the data base was built up, it was noticed that the system became slower and slower. The relationship between the speed with which the system entered each new set of data and the amount of data already loaded was analyzed and projected. It became clear that just loading the complete data base would require a year or so of computer time.

It was evident that it would not be possible in practice to create the complete data base, much less use it. While the response time was a less serious problem, it appeared that it also would become unacceptable long before the entire data base was loaded. Installing larger, sufficiently fast hardware would increase the cost to prohibitively high levels, so that was not a practical alternative. Operational tests also uncovered serious problems in the data base software which sometimes resulted in the wrong data being retrieved and in data becoming effectively lost.

Management was forced to conclude that the project, already well into the implementation phase, was technically infeasible. The project was abandoned.

One can only draw the conclusion that this failure would have been avoided if the technical directors of the project had had a better theoretical grounding. A familiarity with the theoretical aspects of data structures and with the time complexity of algorithms for accessing data structured in the several basic ways would almost certainly have enabled them to anticipate the technical problems long before any significant system development work had been performed—instead of after it had been essentially completed.

A system expands until it collapses.

One company's management decided to have an encompassing software system for production planning and materials control designed and implemented. Work began on the project, but for several reasons, primarily lack of backing and pressure from top management, the project gradually waned into oblivion.

A few years later, it was decided again to implement some sort of similar system. This time, operating management decided to take a different approach. A subsystem of limited scope was identified which, in itself, would be economically justifiable. Later, other subsystems of similar nature could be added on. In this way, progress would be made, step by step, toward the all encompassing system originally planned.

After work on the first subsystem had reached a promising stage, the attention of upper management was drawn to the project. It was decided that its scope should be expanded considerably and that the project team be enlarged accordingly. After a new dynamic start, the enlarged project began to fizzle as key milestones approached. Only one part was completed successfully. While it represented a potentially very useful and valuable basis for other subsystems, it did not yield any significant benefits on its own. It was therefore not utilized in practice by the operating departments concerned.

Again, a lack of consistent, practical objectives seems to have been the major cause of this unsuccessful attempt to develop on application system (see "A data base: a good foundation?", page 39).

An arbitrary restriction in system software

A user contracted for the design and programming of a software system for a specialized business application. The system was to be implemented on his existing computer system. The designer determined early in his analysis that an arbitrary restriction in the computer's file management system prevented him from using the most obvious method for structuring the new application system's data. He therefore selected another method for structuring the data files. The chosen method was described in many computer science text books and was commonly used in various types of system software.

Considerable difficulty and delay then arose during the programming phase. Despite the fact that the programmers were all college graduates who had majored in computer science or mathematics, they were only superficially familiar with the selected method. Finally, however, the system was completed and installed successfully.

Here, an adequate knowledge of the underlying theory of data structure enabled the designer of this system to circumvent what would have otherwise been a very serious obstacle to the successful development of this application system. The lack of such knowledge on the part of some members of the team gave rise to significant difficulties during the programming phase. This case confirms once again the usefulness of a good theoretical foundation in computer science. It also raises a question regarding the quality of some university level computer science programs.

Keep trying until it works.

A free lance programmer contracted to write a particular program for a software house. The experienced programmer was not familiar in detail with all technicalities of the target system. Because a critical area was described ambiguously in the manual, he turned to the software house's specialist for that computer system for clarification. When the specialist could not give a definite answer to his question concerning a commonly used file management function, the programmer asked the specialist how he resolved such problems. The specialist replied, "I just keep trying different possibilities until one works."

The programmer felt uneasy about the risk associated with that approach. Even if it would lead to a solution that would work in all of his test cases, he could not be confident that it would work properly under other conditions that he could not foresee but that would certainly arise sometime during the productive lifetime of his program. Instead of following the system specialist's suggestion, he assumed only what was unambiguously stated in the manual and wrote his program accordingly. While isolated parts of his program may not have been written in the most elegant manner possible, he had confidence in the correctness of his product. In fact, no error was ever discovered in his program after he released it. The same could not be said for other programs in the same system written by the specialist.

Notice the proposed use of the trial and error method in this situation. Despite its shortcomings, despite the known fact that it does not always lead to a solution, it was – and still is – often employed. (See, for example, "Theory simplifies practice" on page 33, in which a programmer used the trial and error approach in an unsuccessful attempt to get his program to exhibit the desired behaviour.)

The software development backlog

A large company asked a group of consultants to recommend improvements to certain operational procedures. Although the company's management recognized that such improvements should involve computer based systems, it was specified from the outset that the consultants' recommendations were not to involve the EDP department's resources in any way. The data processing department was already overloaded with preparations for the replacement of its large computer system in a year's time. Existing plans for new software systems would fully occupy the development staff for at least another year. It would be over two years, therefore, before the development of any new application system could be initiated.

The user always had to wait for a software system while it was being designed, developed and implemented. But in the 1970's, the gap between supply and demand grew (just as in Moc) to the point where the user often had to wait a year or more before the development team could even start to work on his system. Among the reasons for this large and growing gap between available supply and demand are 1) the waste of resources in unsuccessful developmental efforts (see e.g. "An integrated collapse in the new world" on page 34), 2) the misguided diversion of resources (see e.g. "A data base: a good foundation?" on page 39), 3) the quantitatively inadequate provisions for training software developers (see e.g. "Computer programming for freshmen, too" on page 26) and 4) the qualitatively inadequate education of software designers (see "An arbitrary restriction in system software" on page 42 and the next story below).

Computer science education?

The governing board of a university decided that a department of computer science should be established. Initially, the various computer oriented subjects taught in other departments were listed in the university's catalog together under the heading "computer science". This formed the base of the new department.

A number of the professors teaching these courses were strongly encouraged to transfer to the new department. Many were afraid, however, that it would prove to be less than a success – assuming that it ever got off to a real start at all. Unwilling to accept the personal professional risk associated with such a move, several with established reputations overtly and successfully resisted attempts to induce them to join the computer science department. Some others quickly changed their professional postures by ceasing to teach any computer oriented courses for several semesters; instead they taught courses safely within the confines of their old departments, courses having no connection with computer science whatsoever. Those that did transfer to the computer science department were careful to leave open the possibility of returning to their old departments later (many did in fact do so). Attempts to attract full time professors from outside the university into the new department were, for the most part, unsuccessful.

After several years, the computer science "department" was operating more or less successfully, but on a small scale and more as an interdisciplinary committee than as a full-fledged department. The curriculum did not offer a comprehensive treatment of computer science; rather it consisted of a minimal base of computer science to which a collection of several system techniques and various applications had been added.

While this educational program was more extensive than those available one to two decades earlier (see e.g. "Computer programming for freshmen, too" on page 26), it was probably even farther behind what was needed at the time than those earlier courses had been. Even worse, the content of the new courses was much farther behind the state of the art than was the content of the course referenced in "Computer programming for freshmen, too" in its day. In other words, the education of software practitioners is progressing, but much more slowly than it could and should be advancing.

A tale of two operating systems

A microcomputer system was designed and readied for the market. Many observers were surprised when the manufacturer decided to commit the system's new operating system and its interpreter for a high level language to read only memory (ROM). They pointed out that all such software systems contain errors and that releasing a revised version would necessitate hardware modifications to all delivered units, a logistically difficult and very expensive undertaking. These observers were later surprised by the quality of this software – in practice, only one or two truly minor errors were identified and no modification of systems in the field was ever necessary.

The manufacturer later supplied as an accessory disk units together with a disk operating system. This software contained a tremendous number of errors. Not until the fourth version was released did the purchasers have a usable system. Even that version still contained errors, but these did not preclude productive use of the system. In the meantime, independent software suppliers developed and marketed corrected and enhanced versions of the disk operating system. These also had their shortcomings and errors.

These examples illustrate that reasonably complicated software systems of high quality (i.e., essentially error free) *can* be developed in practice – but still we revert to our old ways and turn out shoddy work.

A heuristic program for production planning

The manager of a production planning department asked an EDP specialist with a mathematical bent to investigate the feasibility of optimizing a regularly recurring task of his department. The goal was to schedule the production of a particular type of product so that the amount of scrap generated would be minimized.

The specialist investigated the applicability of several mathematical methods to this problem. He found that all required so much computer time that they were not economically justifiable in the given situation. In the course of his investigation, however, he discovered a simple heuristic method which almost always gave optimum results and always gave better results than the previously used manual method. He programmed the new method on a small microcomputer system which was purchased for this application.

The project cost a few weeks of the specialist's time, a few man days of the time of members of the production planning department and less than $1,000 for the microcomputer. The new system saved about 40% of the time of one production planner and more than 3% of those production costs affected by his planning decisions. The production planner was glad that he could now devote much of his time to other important tasks which he had heretofore been forced to neglect.

Again, the combination of a good foundation in theoretical principles and a good sense of what is needed in practice seems to be associated with success. (See "Sometimes software systems do work – but not by chance." on page 38).

Internally recruited coding technicians

Most of the coding technicians (programmers in the narrow sense) in a data processing department had been recruited from other departments of the company. Their data processing training consisted of a few short courses conducted by one computer manufacturer. They also attended an occasional seminar conducted by external training organizations. Even after a number of years of programming experience, their error rate was high and overall productivity was low. On more than one occasion it had been necessary to scrap man-weeks of programming work and start writing a program anew. Their programs did not exhibit a uniform style or structure and were therefore difficult to maintain and modify.

A consultant who was asked to evaluate the staff's technical competence found that these programmers had never been exposed to a number of fundamental subjects of value in programming, only to technical details of specific software systems. Their lack of exposure to logical (Boolean) algebra, for example, explained many of their errors in writing IF statements. Their lack of familiarity with basic concepts of strings and string operations was an underlying cause of the rigidity designed into some of the application systems they had produced. None knew more than one programming language; most were familiar with only one or two dialects of that language.

It would seem that the training given to a "three week wonder" is simply insufficient in today's software world, just as that type of training was insufficient in Moc in 2400 B.C.

Theory predicts problems in practice.

Several members of the programming staff of a company's data processing department attended a seminar on data and algorithmic structure. Among the topics covered were the interaction between data definition and the overlay structure of a program and, in particular, the problems that could arise if such interaction were not carefully considered when designing the program's structure. Several weeks later, one of the programmers experienced mysterious, erratically occurring problems while testing a program he had just written. After some time, he was able to identify the nature of the problem and to relate it to the material covered in the course. By following suggestions discussed in the course, he was able to solve his problem quickly.

The usefulness of a basic knowledge of computer science theory is again confirmed.

Macroproblems with microsystems

Management of a small distributor of industrial products were dissatisfied with the poor control they had over their inventory. They decided to implement a simple inventory control system using a microcomputer. Preliminary analysis showed that, for their inventory, such a system was technically and economically feasible, but that the limited storage capacity of the diskettes would impose a very severe design constraint. The probable consequences would be "disk jockeying" (the need to remount diskettes frequently) and a certain amount of time overhead for file accessing caused by the need for indexed files with variable length records with variable length fields. It was pointed out that, from a technical standpoint, a small minicomputer configuration would constitute a much better basis for the desired system. Because a suitable minicomputer configuration would have cost very much more than a microcomputer system, however, it was decided to proceed with the microcomputer approach, despite its obvious shortcomings.

The problems began when the hardware was installed. After much trouble shooting, it was discovered that the hardware was unduly sensitive to electrical noise on the power line. Installation of a power line filter and an engineering change to the hardware by the supplier (other installations had experienced the same problem) solved the hardware difficulties.

The first disk operating system supplied by the manufacturer turned out to be very unreliable. A new release worked better but was still unsatisfactory. Finally, a third version was released which solved the problems in the operating system. By this time, however, all data files had become contaminated by the effects of the errors in the earlier versions of the operating system. After several months, the data files were finally restored to a correct state.

The system's useful life finally began. The information which the system provided was of considerable interest and value to management, so their demand for output reports increased considerably. The speed of the system, especially in the file accessing area, became a serious limitation. The report printing programs were therefore modified slightly so that a series of them could be executed overnight in an unattended run. This procedure worked well – only once did the paper jam and cause damage to the printer. The "disk jockeying" represented a distinct inconvenience but was mastered by the users, who had had no previous experience with computer systems.

After the system had been in successful operation for about a year, a compiler was announced for the language in which the application programs were written. In order to speed up one important program in particular, the compiler was purchased. The first attempts to compile the programs failed – the compiler and its associated loader could handle only trivially small programs. In addition, they contained many major errors. A revised version was promised in two months; it was finally delivered about six months late. While it apparently still contained a few less serious errors, it could be used to some extent. In some cases, it was necessary to reduce the size of a program (by eliminating some of its functions) before it could be compiled and loaded.

Except for the lack of programming errors in the application software, all of the classical problems with computer systems (old and new, large and small) arose in connection with this system. Despite the many problems encountered, this application is considered by its users to be, on balance, a successful one. In addition to the improved control over their inventory, the users have gained much useful experience in the application of computer systems to their business activities. They are now much better prepared for their next system than they would be without this experience.

After some two decades, we are still experiencing the same problems and making the same mistakes. (Compare "The disappearing programs" on page 28, "Fully tried and tested?" on page 29, "It works – most of the time" on page 30, etc.) In the case of the microcomputer, though, different people are making them. This suggests that our mechanisms for transmitting knowledge and accumulated experience from one generation of practitioners to the next – i.e., our educational and training programs – are not achieving their objectives. But despite all the difficulties, there is still a net benefit to be derived from utilizing these systems.

A utility's experience with EDP

Just before the decade 1970–1980 began, one utility converted their billing system from an electromechanically supported manual operation to a computer based system. It was expected, of course, that this progressive step would result in a smoothly operating, cost-effective administration of billing and related activities. This expectation turned out to be unrealistically optimistic, even naive.

During the decade 1970–1980, the computerized billing and accounts receivable system was revised five times. Three major revisions were required within one and a half years. Two modifications were accompanied by so much chaos and turmoil that parts of the billing operation became delayed by as much as six months. Two of the revisions required complete replacement of the application software. All but one of the revisions involved reprogramming substantial parts of the software.

This company's experience illustrates that not only do the same problems arise repeatedly in the industry as a whole, the same problems tend also to recur within one organization. Even individuals seem not to be learning from their mistakes.

At the end of the decade, they're still collapsing.

A system was developed in a large corporation for consolidating divisional and regional sales forecasts and for calculating the net requirements of finished goods. The new system was designed and developed in about two years by a team consisting of members of the materials management, production, marketing and EDP departments. After the new system had been in operation for about six months, it was decided that it was unusable in practice. It was, therefore, scrapped.

The user reverted to the old "system" – a collection of programs which had evolved over many years. It was felt that these programs, despite their known shortcomings, satisfied the users' needs better than the new, specially designed system.

To collapse or not to collapse?

A large wholesale distributor contracted with a computer manufacturer for a computer system and specially developed software for a specific business application. The application involved was considered to be of moderate complexity but well within the state of the art. When the hardware was installed, more or less on time, the application software was not yet ready for use. After a few months, the manufacturer released the software to the customer for acceptance testing. The software system failed the test miserably. The manufacturer's software staff worked on the system for some time, after which the acceptance test was repeated. While fewer major problems were discovered during the second test, the system still did not perform satisfactorily. After more rework and a third acceptance test, the customer conditionally approved the system. At the end of the decade, the system was being implemented – more than one year late. The prognosis for success was reasonably good but by no means certain.

The 1980's

Even though the 1980's have only started, there is no dearth of collapses and lesser problems in this decade to relate:

An integrated collapse in the whole world

A world wide transportation company contracted with an important computer manufacturer for the supply of several large computer systems and for the development of customized software for an integrated fleet operations and accounting system. Two years later, shortly before key elements of the system were to be installed, the supplier announced that it had discontinued the project and would not deliver the application software.

After "An integrated collapse in the new world" and "An integrated collapse in the old world" (see pages 34 and 36, respectively), this was bound to happen sooner or later.

A computer work week is shorter than a human work week.

A citizen received a bill from a governmental agency. He did not understand why the small amount was due and telephoned the agency for clarification. A civil servant replied to his request for information, "Our on-line terminals are turned off now. Please call back on a Monday, Wednesday or Friday morning between 8:30 and 12:00." When the citizen called back at one of these times, all telephone lines to that governmental agency were, of course, busy.

This episode begs the question, "Who is there to serve whom – man to serve the machine or the machine to serve man?" Surely the latter, for if the former, then everyone would agree that we should get rid of the machine as quickly as possible. But if the latter, then the machine must be available when needed by man, not when convenient for the machine.

Why is my EDP department so slow?

The president of a corporation asked a consultant, who had just completed a short assignment in one of the functional departments using EDP systems, "Is my EDP department any good? It takes at least two years to get any new system developed and running. And then, more often than not, their systems do not really fulfill our needs. What is wrong? What should I do about it?"

Can a computer system push the button?

A failure in one country's computerized defense control system resulted in a false report of an enemy attack. Interceptors were sent to ward off the attack. Fortunately, the error was discovered before any weapons were launched and armed.

What might have happened if the error had not been discovered until later? To what extent was the possibility of this type of failure properly considered by the system's designers and developers? Did they take all feasible steps to ensure that their software system was as free of errors as possible? Do software practitioners in general give adequate consideration to the possible negative consequences (large and small) of the mistakes they embed in their systems? Because the potential negative consequences of errors in software are becoming ever more serious (compare this episode with "The TOP SECRET blank pages" on page 31), it is becoming increasingly important that all software designers and developers consider these issues more carefully and seriously in the future than they have in the past. If they do not, then other members of society will have to ban them from creating such systems.

Keep trying until it works (2).

A large, hierarchically structured, modular program formed the center of an on-line system being developed for the sales department of a moderately large corporation. When the coder was nearly finished writing all modules in the large program, he tried to link and load them. Not really surprised to see the error message "MEMORY OVERFLOW", he set about defining an overlay structure for the program.

The project manager, who had expected that the program would require overlaying, became concerned when days went by and no promising signs of progress could be discerned. He asked one of the program's designers to look into the matter.

The designer found that the coder – one of the better ones on the project team – had been trying various overlay structures to see if any could be successfully loaded. While the coder had not simply picked combinations at random to try, his approach was something less than systematic. The designer quickly recognized that the number of logically feasible ways of grouping modules into overlay segments was so large that no trial and error approach could be considered a reasonable way to try to solve the problem. It had not even been demonstrated that the problem had a solution, i.e. that an overlay structure existed which would enable the program to fit into memory.

The designer, working together with the coder, collected the relevant data on each module (size and subsidiary module(s) called) and prepared a short program for analyzing this data. A first analysis showed that the program as coded could not be overlayed so that it would fit into memory, i.e. the trial and error approach employed earlier would never have yielded a solution. With this information and knowing the precise amount of memory they had to save, the designer and coder reviewed the program's structure. They noticed that they could reduce the memory requirement sufficiently by redefining certain large data areas local to several modules as global data areas. After this was done, the analysis program was run again. Several adequate overlay structures then became apparent. One which would minimize the reloading of overlay segments during execution was then selected.

The method of trial and error has been used extensively for designing and developing software. This method has stood the test of time very poorly. Often (as in this case and in the episode "Theory simplifies practice" on page 33) it cannot lead to a solution. In other cases (see "Keep trying until it works" on page 43), it all too often leads to a solution which works only some of the time. Despite its shortcomings, the method of trial and error seems to remain popular among software practitioners. Perhaps they know no other way to solve certain problems?

Taxation by computer

A tax office responsible for a large European city implemented a new, computerized system for processing taxpayers' accounts. Many taxpayers, their tax consultants and lawyers described the episode as "chaos". Taxpayers received incorrect tax bills and overdue notices for amounts neither due nor previously billed. The problems were attributed to programming and administrative errors.

Again, innocent persons were forced to suffer the consequences of software developers' mistakes.

The beginnings of an information society?

An individual subscribed to a data communications and data base service. Shortly after receiving his password, he successfully accessed and used the system.

His initial euphoria was soon replaced by a more realistic awareness of the true nature of the computer and software world. Two days later, he tried to access the system again. Repeatedly, he was refused access by the system. He called a customer service representative, who informed him that during a revision of the network's software the night before, a number of subscribers' entries had been inadvertently deleted from the system. A few hours later, his user number and password had been reentered and he could access the system again.

If such experiences are typical of the difficulties to which members of the general public will be exposed when computer based public services are introduced over the next years, we should not be surprised when public acceptance is poor. Society has become accustomed to a certain level of reliability of other common, technologically based services, for example, the supply of water and electricity, telephone service, automobiles, home appliances, television, etc. Until the reliability of services based on computer technology reaches a comparably high level, we cannot expect the public to avail itself of those services. Until computer based services become sufficiently reliable, society cannot afford to let itself become dependent upon them.

*Software failure **can** bankrupt a company.*

A small wholesale distributor of office supplies and equipment purchased a minicomputer system with application software from an established computer manufacturer. The salesmen assured the customer that their system was capable of performing the functions the customer required in the invoicing, accounts receivable, accounts payable and accounting areas.

The system was installed. Within a short time, essentially all of the customer's administration in the above mentioned areas was "on the computer". After a few months, problems arose. Difficulties with the system resulted in delays in invoicing customers and in paying suppliers. The situation became progressively worse and the company finally became insolvent.

While one can, did and will argue about whether the computer system or imprudent management was the real reason for the bankruptcy, there is no denying that the failure of the application software to perform as promised by the salesmen and as expected by the customer contributed to this company's difficulties and its ultimate downfall.

Software improvements?

A software system for the consolidation and rebilling of invoices was designed, programmed and implemented in an organization which functioned as an invoice clearing house. After the normal errors and problems were overcome during the immediate post-implementation phase, the system was used without major mishap for almost two years.

Then, suddenly, the main operational file was found to be in an inconsistent state and unusable by the system. The several daily generations of this file which were maintained by the normal security procedures were all incorrect. For more than a week, the clearing house was unable to rebill the amounts due and was forced to request payments on account from the purchasers of the goods involved.

An investigation of the situation was conducted. It was discovered that a short time before the problem arose, an erroneous revision had been made to a program which updated the file and a hardware failure had occurred. While it was not possible to identify with certainty the true cause of the loss of the file, it appeared probable that the error in the revision to the program was to blame.

The consequences of this error on the cash flow of this organization were considerable, not to mention the much increased workload on the people in the billing and accounting departments. The organization had become totally dependent upon the computer system and that system was out of service for more than a week. One wonders if the software practitioner who had inadvertently caused the failure was aware of the severity of the possible consequences of his error. Are software practitioners in general consciously and adequately aware of the heavy responsibility they often carry? Do they realize how severe the consequences of their carelessness or insufficient attention to detail can be?

Better late than never

Management in a moderately large company approved a proposal to develop an on-line system for the marketing and sales department. The development project involved designing, programming and implementing application software as well as selecting and installing minicomputer equipment. Based on specific assumptions which were well documented by the project manager, the initial development plan called for implementation to take place nine to ten months after the detailed design effort started. This project, one of the more successful larger system development efforts undertaken by the company's EDP department in years, was finally completed fifteen months late.

The reasons for the slippage were identified as conflicts in resource allocation, overly optimistic estimates of the time required to complete the various individual activities in the project and low programmer productivity. Several times, a program coder was taken off the project without warning to correct or modify an old, operational program which did not function as required. Usually, he returned to the development project in a few weeks. In one or two cases, however, the coder never was reassigned to the project. In other cases, a coder was scheduled to join the development project team after completing another assignment but, in fact, never did.

These problems were not new in this decade. They have been with us for decades. We seem not to be learning from any of our mistakes, be they technical or managerial in nature.

Computers work to rule.

On one data communications and data base network, the computers on which some data bases are resident work only eight hours a day, five days a week. Perhaps their programmers have endowed them with a mind of their own so that the machines have outside interests and have raised themselves above the level of slaves. Or have their programmers simply been unable to endow these systems with the ability to operate reliably for some hours without human assistance?

If computer based services of widespread interest are to become accepted and commonplace, they – like other utilities – must be available at all times. (See "The beginnings of an information society?" on page 54.)

Out of service

When a major revision to the software in a data communications system was installed, the entire network was inoperative for several days. The network had been in operation for over one year when this interruption of service occurred.

Again, this episode raises serious questions regarding the reliability and availability of publicly accessible information networks. One wonders how seriously the system's designers and developers take these social requirements. Or do the demands of developing these systems simply exceed their technical abilities?

Better late than never (2)

A large transportation company contracted with a computer manufacturer for the supply of a computer system. The system included specially developed application software for the reservation of vehicles and space thereon and for related operational functions. The software system centered around a large scale data bank.

The manufacturer quoted a delivery time of two years. The actual delivery time was more than four years.

Better late than never (3)

A governmental agency contracted with a computer manufacturer for an air traffic control system for a region including a very busy commercial airport. The planned development time was two years; the actual development time was more than four years.

The delay was attributed to ineffective communication between the system's designers and users within the customer's organization. This led to a less than adequate specification for the system. This, in turn, resulted in minor disagreements between the supplier and the customer over the meaning of various passages in the specification. Finally, delays were caused by the unwillingness of the quality control manager to approve some sections of the software when originally submitted by the programming and testing teams.

The same, decades old problems continue to arise in developmental projects.

Computer programming for high school freshmen

In several high schools with good academic reputations, computing courses were offered for students in all grades. Whereas the teachers of biology, chemistry, physics, history, social studies, languages, mathematics, etc., had all studied their subjects for several years in college, the teachers of the computing class had had only brief contact with their subject in college. The better prepared teachers had taken computing courses for one or two semesters in college; others had learned the rudiments of programming within the framework of another course.

While the students were expected to delve into the grammatical structure of natural languages, they were not expected to become familiar with the syntactical rules of the programming language they were learning. While they were expected to be able to prove the Pythagorean theorem, to prove that the square root of two is not a rational number and to derive the quadratic formula, they were not expected to be able to prove that the algorithms they specified and the programs they wrote did anything in particular, much less that they did something correctly. While they were expected to be able to organize their essays clearly and logically, they were not expected to be able to structure their programs in a similar manner. In short, lower standards of quality were set for their work in computing courses than in other classes.

Not only universities initiate substandard educational programs for software related subjects (see "Computer science education?" on page 00). Now, secondary schools are experiencing the same difficulties – and making the same mistakes.

The seminar for experienced software designers

An international organization arranged a seminar on advanced methods for designing and developing algorithms and computer programs. Among the lecturers engaged to conduct the seminar were some of the world's recognized leaders in the field. Both academicians and advanced practitioners were invited to apply for admission to the seminar.

The number of applications greatly exceeded the expectations of the organizers and, of course, the planned capacity. It was necessary to reject a very considerable number of well qualified applicants.

Where shall we get the teachers?

Many educators have experienced considerable difficulty in attracting qualified persons into college teaching careers in the computer science field. Many reasons have been cited for the reluctance especially of new Ph.D. graduates to choose careers in academia. The salaries offered by colleges and universities are not competitive with those offered by industry. Industrial research laboratories are usually better equipped than those in academic institutions. The administrative burden on the academic researcher is often perceived to be heavier than that on his industrial colleague.

The result is that many planned faculty positions go unfilled. In turn, many needed faculty positions probably go unplanned. Our current severe shortage of academically trained software engineers is likely to continue – if not get worse.

When one compares these last two situations with the lack of instructors in "Computer programming for freshmen, too" (page 26), it is evident that we have made surprisingly little progress in the last two to three decades. Does this mean that we are really no better off now than we were in the 1950's? Will the next decades be qualitatively much like the last decades? Have we, like ostriches, had our heads buried in the sand all this time? How much longer will we leave them there?

The state of software affairs today

As stated earlier, the preceding narratives understate the successes of the software producing sector of our society. Obviously, there have been successes – substantial successes – which more than offset the negative consequences outlined above. But anyone who has been involved for any length of time in producing or using software systems will find many of the true situations described above to be representative of his own experiences. The problems, difficulties and shortcomings outlined above are not the exceptions, they are, unfortunately, the rule.

Is this the picture of a profession or an industry fulfilling its social responsibility? If it is trying, it does not appear to be succeeding very well. One can only conclude that most practitioners either are acting irresponsibly or – more probably – are simply underqualified for the tasks they are attempting to perform.

Is this the picture of a society making optimum use of the programmers of its computers? The qualitatively and quantitatively inadequate initial education of these resources alone prevents them from making an optimum contribution to their employers and to their fellow man. The moderate amount of on-going technical training does not, cannot compensate for the inadequate development of their capabilities. Not only the programmers of our computers but also our business, intellectual, political and social leadership is inadequately prepared for the task of ensuring that society takes optimum advantage of computer technology.

Who is to blame? Everyone and no one. Everyone concerned with software – directly and indirectly – has contributed to the current state of affairs. But because this situation has become, tacitly at least, accepted business practice, no one group can be singled out as the culprits. Certainly one cannot blame our many "three week wonders", for they have responded to the market demand and to the challenge in greater numbers than any other group. Considering the cursory preparation they have been given, they have, for the most part, tried hard and performed well. But more of them should be motivated, encouraged and helped to upgrade their base of fundamental, general knowledge of computer science topics and of relevant background subjects.

It is interesting to compare the above state of affairs in the software field with the situation prevailing in the computer hardware field. The hardware field, from its very beginning a recognized engineering discipline, has succeeded in developing sophisticated, reliable equipment. The computer industry has succeeded in producing it in large quantities. The reliability and capacity of typical hardware systems have been increasing at an almost unbelievable rate for many years. At the same time, the cost of hardware has been declining rapidly. These trends are certain to continue for years to come. While the collapse rate in the hardware field is not zero, it is much, much lower than that in the software field.

It is striking that the developers of computer hardware are academically trained engineers. The academic programs for these engineers evolved naturally from already well established courses of study in electrical engineering. The evolution took place for the most part within existing, relatively large departments of electrical engineering at recognized academic institutions. It was not necessary to found new departments and faculties in order to establish the organizational base for sound engineering programs in computer hardware development.

In the software field, academia has experienced much greater problems. No established base existed upon which software engineering could grow in a natural way. While important roots existed in the mathematics and electrical engineering departments, software engineering differs in fundamental ways from both of these fields. At the same time, other academic fields are also of considerable importance to the software engineer, namely those dealing with the various application areas. Thus, an academic program in the software area must borrow heavily from a number of other academic disciplines but is sufficiently different from each that none provides a base for its evolutionary development. This has given rise to a basic dilemma. It is not clear just how this new field should be fitted organizationally into the academic world. Several alternatives are still being tried. It remains to be seen which will pass the test of time.

Striking differences also exist between the attitudes of those persons responsible for selecting designers of hardware and software systems. It is customary that a prospective hardware designer have an engineering education. If he does not, he is expected to demonstrate that he possesses equivalent knowledge and experience. Lacking this, he may be engaged as a technician or designer's assistant, but not in a designing capacity. In the software field, the situation is very different. Any previous experience, almost regardless of quality and length, is implicitly assumed to be a more than adequate preparation for designing software systems. Seldom is a prospective software system designer expected to have fulfilled any particular formal educational requirements. This is particularly true in the case of software for business applications – probably the largest segment of the software market. While the persons selecting these designers are not really satisfied with the results, they do not, in their view, have any other choice. Truly qualified software designers are simply not available in the quantities needed.

Another important attitudinal difference contributes to the maintenance of the status quo. From the earliest days of computing, the purchaser has subconsciously felt that what he was really buying was the hardware. The software was a minor accessory. This attitude probably reflected the cost structure of computer systems in the 1940's and early 1950's reasonably well. Beginning in the late 1950's and during the 1960's and the 1970's, however, the cost of a typical computer system was more or less balanced between hardware and software. For a long time, however, the industry's pricing policy did not reflect this cost structure and the typical computer user still had the impression that he was buying the valuable hardware and getting the cheap software as an accessory.

Today, the sophisticated user realizes that the solution to his problem lies not in the hardware but in the software. Starting from his problem, he determines his software requirements. Only then does he select the hardware required to execute the software. He is really buying the software; the hardware is the accessory.

Even when the user consciously recognizes this fact, his subconscious, however, still often perceives the hardware to be the object being purchased and the software to be the unimportant accessory. There is an understandable reason for this psychological effect. To every human being, even software experts, computer hardware is more tangible than software. The very choice of the words "hardware" and "software" can be attributed to this common human perception. The more tangible thing, having more substance, is perceived subjectively to be of greater value. While software takes on tangible forms, its essence is perceived as largely intangible and hence of less intrinsic value. The person who subconsciously and genuinely recognizes that software is the real good being purchased and that the hardware is only a minor accessory has managed to overcome a deeply ingrained aspect of his human psychology.

According to an established rule of thumb in software production, testing (a euphemism for finding and correcting mistakes) accounts for about half of the development effort of a typical software system [McGowan, p. 2], [Myers, p. vii], [Schulz, p. 9]. The remaining half is divided unequally between program design and coding. After development is pronounced complete, considerable additional cost – often more than the development cost – is incurred during the system's lifetime for maintenance (i.e. finding and correcting mistakes not found during testing, implementing design changes and finding and correcting mistakes introduced thereby). The very large amount of effort expended in "testing" should be an unmistakable signal that something is *fundamentally* wrong with our approach to designing and coding program systems. Apparently, however, this message is not getting through to the programmers of our computers. The high cost of testing seems to have spawned valiant efforts to develop and refine tools and techniques for testing – rather than to get our designs and code right in the first place. In other words, the medicine we are taking will (if it works) give us symptomatic relief from our ills but will not cure us.

Why has the state of affairs reflected by the preceding narratives become the socially accepted modus operandi? The computer is a fundamentally new tool so useful that even when sloppily applied by beginners and amateurs, the net benefit – after due consideration of the collapses – is still very great. The benefits are so great in the short term that we cannot economically and socially justify foregoing them while we take time out to prepare ourselves to take better advantage of this new tool in the future.

While we can be proud of the abilities we have acquired and of the positive results we have so far achieved, we must beware of unjustified self-laudation and its likely consequences. Our successes should not be interpreted to mean that we are doing a good job, but rather that we have, more or less by accident, stumbled onto a good thing. We could and should endeavour to make much more of this good thing in the future than we are now doing.

What is wrong with the current situation?

Because the net benefits are so great, one might ask, "What is really so bad about the current state of affairs? We are producing large quantities of software which is of considerable value to its users. As long as this situation prevails, we don't *really* have a problem." Perhaps the potentially worst aspect of the current situation is illustrated by the two narratives regarding defense applications. As our systems become bigger, better and more beneficial, so does the potential damage resulting from their failure become more serious. While the "TOP SECRET blank pages" (page 31) in the 1960's constituted a ludicrous situation involving only a little waste and certainly no danger, the episode "Can a computer system push the button?" (page 52) represents a potentially very dangerous situation. While no one really objected to his bank account being processed by computer ten years ago, many people might justifiably object to flying in an aircraft whose route will be monitored and controlled solely by computer software of the same quality as that in the preceding stories. The damage done by software failures in the past was almost always reversible; in the future, it is likely that more and more irreversible damage will be done if we continue on our present path.

There are other negative consequences of our current approach to the programming of our computers. From a simple economic standpoint, the main shortcoming is the considerable gap between supply and demand in the software market. More generally, we are paying unnecessarily high costs for our software and its use and we are obtaining less benefit than possible. We too often incur avoidable costs as a result of errors and failures. Such costs are sometimes shifted unfairly onto persons who are not responsible for the errors and failures that cause them, onto persons who have no control over the situation and onto persons who cannot protect themselves from the consequences of such errors and failures. For example, many taxpayers lost considerable time and incurred legal fees as a consequence of "Taxation by computer" (page 54). In many similar situations customers of an organization whose software has malfunctioned have been inconvenienced and have incurred costs and lost time in correcting the mistakes. Even when the costs to any one person are low, the total economic loss can be high when the number of persons affected is large – as is often the case.

Another negative consequence of our present approach to computer education seems to be receiving too little attention. The ability to use and to interact meaningfully with information systems is becoming more and more important to the individual as a productive element in society. Those who do not acquire basic skills in the use of informational tools of various types are likely to be at a disadvantage in our future society, much as those who cannot read, write, perform basic arithmetic operations or drive an automobile are at a considerable disadvantage today. If we do not start conveying basic "informational skills" to all our children in the schools soon, a substantial fraction of the next few generations may be "computer illiterate". The opportunity costs associated with such a situation would be high, to say nothing of the potential social conflict that could arise from the attendant polarization of society into the informationally poor and the informationally rich.

Why do we have severe software problems?

Why do we have such serious problems in the software field today? The immediate answer is, of course, simple and obvious: we have too few programmers and the ones we do have are not as good as we would like. Right now, we appear to need every living, breathing programmer we can get – almost regardless of quality. While marginally qualified practitioners are normally squeezed out of a field by economic and competitive forces, these forces are more than counteracted in today's software market by the large gap between supply and demand. Marginal practitioners are seldom forced out of the software market; instead they move on to another employer (and receive an increase in pay in the process, of course).

Just as in Moc in 2400 B.C., we have simultaneously a shortage of quantity and quality. This shortage stems, in the final analysis, from a bottleneck in the educational process. The bottleneck, caused fundamentally by the rapid growth of the computer field, is aggravated by our concentration on short term benefits. In order to obtain maximum benefit now, we are diverting valuable resources from the education of tomorrow's programmers of our computers. Potential teachers are engaged as practitioners or in research; potential students of computer science are engaged as poorly prepared "system analysts" and coding technicians today and tomorrow instead of as good software engineers tomorrow.

Many failures of software projects have been attributed to managerial error. Within the context of individual projects and systems, managerial errors have frequently been a contributing cause of our many collapses. When unrealistic goals and expectations are set, when the ability of the organization to design, develop, implement and absorb software systems is greatly overestimated, when a software project is initiated (or allowed to continue) which requires more highly qualified people than those assigned to the project team, then management must accept responsibility for the ensuing collapse. But managerial misjudgment is only one of several causes of our problems. These managerial errors hardly explain the large gap between our practical ability to realize software systems on the one hand and what we know can be achieved in principle on the other hand. They do not adequately explain why highly qualified people are in such short supply or why the available people are not better qualified. They do not explain why the total supply of software practitioners is so much less than the demand.

Managerial misjudgment is only an intermediate expression of more fundamental causes of our problems. We must ask further why business leaders commit these errors. All too often, they are not adequately aware of the possibilities and limitations of computer technology as it can be applied in business and society. Often unclear to them is the important distinction between what one can in principle achieve on the one hand and what a particular group of people can achieve in a particular organization within a limited period of time on the other hand. Euphoria over what is possible in principle often leads to unrealistic expectations; then the resulting collapse causes the pendulum to swing to the other extreme and their attitudes become overly pessimistic and excessively conservative. Good advice based on sound knowledge of the technical possibilities and limitations is not always available. When it is, the manager is not always in a position to recognize good and bad advice as such and to distinguish between the two. When faced with a choice between foregoing a software system because qualified developers are not available or trying to develop it with underqualified staff, the decision process is all too often dominated by the hope that this time everything will somehow work out all right. Often, of course, it doesn't and the net result is that resources already in short supply are wasted.

The shortage of qualified software practitioners is further aggravated by frequent conversions of a technical nature. Considerable manpower is required to convert from one computer system to another, from one operating system to another, from batch to on-line operation, from traditional file management systems to data base management systems, etc. While most such conversions are motivated by the expectation of increased productivity, too frequently they consume more resources than they free.

In an attempt to circumvent the shortage of qualified software practitioners, we have, often quite consciously, tried to deskill programming. This has only made matters worse. By creating the impression that programming requires only minimal skill, we have discouraged many highly capable persons from becoming programmers and have encouraged too many with marginal aptitude to join the ranks of coders. This effect is particularly noticeable in some European countries, where until recently it was socially unacceptable to place a college graduate in the position of a "programmer". The low quality of the resulting software should not surprise anyone. If we were to deskill aircraft piloting, we would expect an increase in crashes and lesser accidents. If we were to deskill the task of civil engineers, we would expect an increase of Mocsian collapses. If we were to deskill the task of the physician, we would expect an increase in diagnostic errors, surgical deaths, misuse of medicines, inappropriate therapy, etc. Having deskilled programming, we are observing the comparable consequences.

By deskilling programming, we have drawn attention away from the programmers' need for a solid base of fundamental knowledge. Instead of emphasizing a fundamental understanding of the nature of information and information processing, we have been stuffing the programmer full of unorganized and often confusing technical details of this or that system. Over and over again, we have searched for a kit bag of the right tools, with which the most difficult problems could be solved simply and easily. At best, this has been like Ponce de Leon's legendary search for the fountain of youth: while the goal was not achieved, useful by-products derived from the effort. But all too often our searches for the right tools have been more akin to a search for the pot of gold at the end of the rainbow: much effort has been expended and no useful results have been achieved. Still other efforts have been quixotic adventures.

All too often, the "technical details" of the software system being learned are nothing more than the arbitrary and unnecessary restrictions imbedded into it by its creators. The new programmer is soon deluded into mistaking such technical details of a system for true knowledge of general applicability. This sort of training does not broaden his mental horizons; on the contrary, it narrows them. Instead of improving the capabilities of the next generation of programmers, this type of training tends to pass on to them our inabililties rather than our abilities and thereby to perpetuate undesirable aspects of the status quo.

As promising new tools turn out not to solve all our needs after all, confusion often sets in. After much discussion and some investigation, the proponents announce that the tool is fine, but that it is not being applied properly. The search then begins for the right technique for applying the tool and the vicious cycle begins again. This process is very much like the situation in which the programmer was unknowingly trying to program the unprogrammable (see "Theory simplifies practice", page 33). As one difficulty is resolved, another pops up to take its place. We seem to be unwilling to face up to the obvious conclusion: specific tools and techniques can complement, but never replace a fundamental understanding of the nature and structure of the problem.

In this context, it is interesting to ask how many of the programmers of our computers are graduates of a university level computer ,science program. While the various sets of statistics relevant to this topic are problematical, in part because of definitional difficulties, it is clear that only a very small fraction of our programmers have studied computer science in any depth. In the U.S.A., some 29,600 bachelor's degrees were awarded in computer and information sciences in the six year period 1972–1977 [U.S. Bureau of the Census, p. 169]. These courses of study were first offered in the 1960's and are still growing; therefore it can be assumed that in all years before 1972, at most a comparable number of such degrees were awarded. The number of master's degrees and doctorates awarded is undoubtedly even smaller. These numbers are quite small in comparison with the number of active programmers (in our sense of the word) – certainly many hundreds of thousands, if not a million or more in the U.S.A.

In the Federal Republic of Germany, the European country with the largest market for computer equipment and services, the situation is similar. According to governmental statistics, 10,851 students entered university level courses of study in computer science ("Informatik") in the five years 1974–1978 [Statistisches Bundesamt, p. 342, and earlier editions]. Until the early 1970's, such courses of study were essentially unknown. The number of programmers (again, in our sense of the word) in the F.R.G. is certainly several hundred thousand.

In addition to graduates of computer science programs, there are, of course, many graduates of other courses of study who are performing programming functions. While some of these have acquired a knowledge of computer science subjects, it is probably fair to say that most have acquired only a technical knowledge of one or two programming languages and one or two computer systems. While many of them may be engineers in other fields, only relatively few can be considered to be programming or software engineers.

Often it is assumed – sometimes implicitly, sometimes explicitly – that the difficult, critical aspects of designing, developing and implementing a software system lie in the area of EDP technicalities. A system analyst is therefore assigned to some particular project who is familiar with the technical idiosyncracies of standard software package X. A coder is selected for the project on the basis of his knowledge of compiler Y and operating system Z. The system analyst conducts a few superficial interviews with the user, designs the software system, passes on corresponding instructions to the coder and defines the data to be collected by the user.

It should not, but usually does, surprise everyone that the resulting system does not perform meaningfully – in terms of the users' needs. What has happened? Specialists in computer systems X and Y and Z have been assigned to design, for example, a system for forecasting sales and optimizing inventories of finished and semi-finished goods. But they are not aware of the business economics involved; they are not familiar with the cost structure of manufacturing and inventory systems. They do not have the mathematical background needed to cope with the statistical questions which arise in sales forecasting or to determine which, if any, of the many inventory optimization models in the theoretical literature might apply to their company's situation. They are not intimately familiar with the unique operational problems, personal preferences, prejudices and political forces existing in the using organization. As a result, they are all too often unable to recognize the users' real informational needs.

The designers of such a software system must apply relevant business theories, mathematics and computer systems (hardware and software) to the tasks of a specific organizational unit in their company. Of these four important areas, they are seldom masters of more than one. Because neither the user nor the computer specialist speaks a language the other understands, communication is ineffective. Instead of a dialog, two (or more) monologs are conducted. Because the computer specialist understands neither the business theory nor the mathematics behind the various formulae in the book from which he hopes to select his solution, no real communication takes place between him and these vast bodies of knowledge, either. The final system will run on a computer, but whether it represents a solution to the user's real problem or not is a completely different matter.

What are we doing in effect? To solve a problem or to perform a task which we don't really understand, we design and build a computerized system (which we don't fully understand, either). Implicitly we assume or hope that the omnipotent computer will somehow compensate for the gaps in our understanding. Of course, it doesn't – because it can't. The only thing surprising under these circumstances is that we actually expect the system to do something useful.

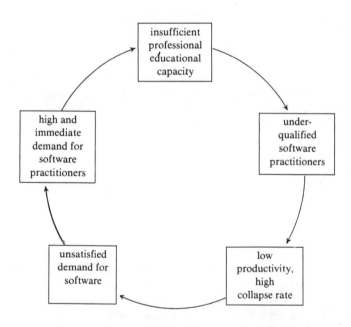

Our contemporary vicious circle

Chapter 3

A test for practitioners of the science/art/craft/trade/racket of software design and development

> *Ignorance, when voluntary, is criminal, and a man may be properly charged with that evil which he neglected or refused to learn how to prevent.*
>
> Samuel Johnson (1709–1784)

> *Pure mathematics do remedy and cure many defects in the wit and faculties of individuals; for if the wit be dull, they sharpen it; if too wandering, they fix it; if too inherent in the sense, they abstract it.*
>
> Francis Bacon (1561–1626)

It is a thesis of this book that there is no kit bag of a few tools and techniques which, if learned and applied by the programmer, will ensure his success. The software engineer must first master a certain body of fundamental knowledge consisting of ideas and concepts selected from the fields of computer science and mathematics. This body of knowledge deals with the basic nature of data, the structure and properties of algorithms and the interaction between data and algorithmic processes. Only after mastering this body of knowledge will the software engineer be able to apply the many available tools and techniques properly and meaningfully – and be able to develop new tools and techniques himself when the need arises.

The questions in the following test have been selected to emphasize

such basic, fundamental knowledge rather than the many specific techniques and the idiosyncracies of typical contemporary software systems.
This is not meant to imply that skill in the use of such techniques and an
awareness of the specific characteristics of typical software systems are
not important to the programmer; they obviously are. While they are
necessary, they are not sufficient, however. The accent on fundamental
concepts in the following exercises is an attempt to rectify the current
overemphasis on specifics and underemphasis on the understanding of
fundamentals.

The knowledge required by the successful programmer of our computers encompasses computer oriented technical subjects, basic mathematics, planning and management of software projects and the application area(s) for which he develops software. The following exercises deal
primarily with the first two of these. Project planning and management is
dealt with in only a brief, introductory manner because little in this area
is really unique to software engineering. Software engineering is but one
of many areas of application of the well known, well documented and
empirically verified principles of project planning and management.
Because the areas to which software systems are applied are so numerous
and so different in nature, they are not dealt with at all in the following
exercises.

Even within the areas of basic computer science and mathematics, this
set of exercises does not purport to be exhaustive. The author's intention
is that it be illustrative of typical basic principles and of the usefulness to
the programmer of a good foundation in basic mathematics. Additional
exercises on computer subjects can be found in [Knuth, Vols. 1, 2 and 3]
and [ACM].

Why is mathematics so important to the programmer? As anyone who
has ever worked with computer systems knows, they are sticklers for
detail. When studying, talking about and designing data structures,
algorithms and programs for computer systems, it is essential that we pay
particular attention to precision and rigorous logic in our discourses. We
need a language which permits, even encourages, precise and logical
expression. We need a language which discourages, even prevents, vague
and fuzzy thinking and expression. The language of mathematics has
been developed over the millennia to fulfill just these needs; it seems to
fulfill them well. While we could, in principle, create some other language
of discourse, there would seem to be no good reason to reinvent the

wheel. We will, therefore, make free use of the language of mathematics – supplemented with some computer terminology – in the following questions and answers. It should be noted that it is not so much the content of the field of mathematics as the *language* of mathematics which is of interest and importance to us as programmers.

Why is mathematics so important to the field of software development? In order to answer this question, it is useful to consider the typical evolution of scientific fields such as astronomy, biology, chemistry, medicine, physics, etc. They all seem to have begun with superstition surrounding a class of phenomena of practical significance to mankind (e.g. astrology, alchemy, etc.). In a second phase, the phenomena were observed intensively. Afterwards, the voluminous collection of observations was organized, structured and analyzed. Numerous hypotheses were formulated; predictions derived from them were compared with the observations. In this third phase, an understanding of the phenomena, their causes and their implications was developed – and the field became a science. In the fourth phase, this understanding was applied, at man's will, to modify his environment, at least to some limited extent.

The key factor enabling the transition through the first phase – superstition – seems to be man's innate psychological need to explain his environment. During the second phase – observation – technical skills in observing, measuring and recording dominate. A key prerequisite for the transition through the third phase – understanding – is a formal language and structure for thinking which enables one to draw rigorously logical conclusions from given or assumed facts or observations – i.e., precisely what we call mathematics today. In the fourth phase – application – creative abilities become essential. These prerequisites are cumulative in the sense that in each phase not only its special prerequisite is employed, but also those of preceding phases.

The field of software development as it is typically practiced today represents a schismatic situation: We are trying to act as if we were in the fourth phase although most practitioners have not, in fact, even made a good start into the third phase. (Some are still stuck in the first phase.) Only when a large fraction of our practitioners has acquired the prerequisite for tackling the third phase will we make significant progress. Only then can our field mature and join the ranks of other scientific and engineering disciplines.

Some readers may find that the exercises below expose gaps in their knowledge of the language of mathematics. It is suggested that they review introductory material on set theory and functions. A familiarity with basic mathematical terminology and a few elementary definitions in these areas will be sufficient background for answering the questions below. Such material can be found in the introductory chapters of many modern books on algebra, real analysis, measure theory, probability theory, functional analysis, etc. See e.g. [Brady, Appendix A], [Harrison, chapter 1] or [Royden, chapter 1].

Answers to the following exercises will be found in the Mocpendium of selected software engineering topics beginning on page 133. If the reader is not able to answer a question, it is suggested that he look up the answer and go on to the next exercise.

The reader who has difficulty with some of these questions should not feel bad; he is not alone. Few software practitioners will be able to answer all the following questions completely and with ease. But because material in all areas covered in this test has been found to be either of direct relevance to common practical problems or of significant value as background knowledge, the reader should polish up his knowledge of those areas in which he experienced difficulty. He should consult the literature referenced in the answers to the questions which he found difficult as well as other pertinent sources. If he has difficulty reading the material referenced, he should work on improving his fluency in the language of mathematics as suggested above.

Good luck!

Questions

Data and algorithms: basic concepts, definitions and axioms

1.1. What is a variable or a data element?
1.2. What is meant by the *type* of a variable or data element?
1.3. What is an array? a subscripted variable?
1.4. Define the word "algorithm".
1.5. What is a data environment (e.g. of an algorithm)?
1.6. What is a computational task?
1.7. What is a data declaration?
1.8. What is an assignment statement?

1.9. What is a *global* variable? a *local* variable? an *own* variable?

1.10. What is a conditional statement?

1.11. What is a WHILE statement?

1.12. The FOR statement is a loop control statement which appears in several programming languages. Define its basic form in terms of the WHILE statement.

1.13. What is a linear list?

1.14. Explain what a linked linear list is.

1.15. What is a stack?

1.16. What is a *recursive* algorithm? Give an example of one.

Automata

2.1. Describe in general terms what a Turing machine is.

2.2. Give a precise definition of a finite automaton.

2.3. When are two finite automata equivalent?

2.4. What is a von Neumann machine?

Boolean algebra

3.1. What is Boolean algebra?

3.2. Define the AND function. Is it associative? commutative?

3.3. Define the OR function. Is it associative? commutative?

3.4. Define the NOT function.

3.5. Are the expressions

NOT (x AND y)

and

(NOT x) OR (NOT y)

equal for all possible values of x and y? If so, prove. If not, give a counterexample.

3.6. Are the expressions

NOT (x OR y)

and

(NOT x) AND (NOT y)

equal for all possible values of x and y? If so, prove. If not, give a counterexample.

3.7. Are the conditional statements

a. IF x THEN statement1 ELSE statement2
b. IF NOT x THEN statement2 ELSE statement1

equivalent? If so, give a precise proof. If not, give a counterexample.

3.8. Show that the statements

a. IF x AND y THEN statement1 ELSE statement2
b. IF (NOT x) OR (NOT y) THEN statement2 ELSE statement1

are equivalent.

3.9. In a program, the elements of two arrays, lastname and firstname, are to be sorted. Write the Boolean expressions for use in IF statements to determine whether the entry with subscript i

a. is lower (less) than the entry with subscript j,
b. is higher (greater) than the entry with subscript j or
c. is equal to the entry with subscript j.

3.10. A programmer wrote the following nested IF statement:

```
IF x
THEN statement1
ELSE IF y
        THEN statement1
        ELSE statement2
```

Simplify this statement. Prove that your simplified statement is equivalent to the above.

Algorithms: implementation, execution and correctness

4.1. How are recursive algorithms executed on real machines?
4.2. What does the following algorithm do? Under what conditions does it do it correctly? What is varying in the loop? More importantly, what is *not* varying during the execution of the loop? Give a detailed proof.

```
sum ← 0
i ← 0
WHILE i < n DO {i ← i + 1; sum ← sum + x(i)}
```

4.3. State the conditions for which the following algorithm is correct. Prove that it computes the desired result.

FUNCTION factorial(n);
IF n = 0
THEN return 1 as the value of factorial
ELSE return the value of n * factorial(n − 1)
    as the value of factorial;

4.4. What can be said about the behaviour of the above algorithm if the value of the argument is a non-integral positive number? a negative number?

4.5. What types of data values can be sorted?

4.6. Describe in general terms the sorting method called "quicksort" due to C. A. R. Hoare.

4.7. Write an algorithm for quicksort. (Assume that a suitable algorithm exists for subdividing the collection of values to be sorted into two subcollections.)

4.8. What requirements must the algorithm satisfy which subdivides the collection of keys to be sorted?

4.9. Prove that your algorithm for quicksort is correct.

4.10. Suggest a loop invariant for the main loop in the algorithm which will subdivide the collection of key values to be sorted.

4.11. Design the algorithm for subdividing the collection of key values to be sorted.

4.12. Prove the correctness of your algorithm for subdividing the collection of key values.

4.13. Write a non-recursive algorithm for quicksort. (Use the previously designed algorithm for subdividing the collection of key values to be sorted.)

4.14. Prove the correctness of your non-recursive algorithm.

4.15. A program is to be written which will print a report with an unspecified number of pages. Each page will contain a header and a footer. The page number will be printed in both the header and the footer. In some cases, a group of a small number of successive lines of data must be printed on the same page. Specify precisely the criteria for the correctness of the format of such a report.

4.16. Design a set of algorithms for controlling the paging and the printing of the header and footer for this report. Specify the control variables required and their exact meanings. Assume only that system functions are available for printing one line and for skipping a specified number of lines.

4.17. In a particular application, a number may be represented by an optional sign, followed by one or more decimal digits, followed optionally by a decimal point and one or more decimal digits. Describe precisely the syntax of such a number using BNF (Backus -Naur-Form) notation.

4.18. Design an algorithm which determines whether a given string of characters satisfies the above definition of a number.

4.19. Names are to be abbreviated as follows. The letter H is to be disregarded unless it is the first letter in the name. A sequence of consonants is to be abbreviated by the first consonant. Similarly, a sequence of vowels is to be abbreviated by the first vowel. Finally, certain letters are to be replaced as follows when they appear within the name (but not as the first letter):

Replace	with
e, i, y	e
b, p	b
c, k, s	c
d, t	d
g, j	g
m, n	m
v, w	v

For example, the abbreviation of JOHANSSON is JOMOM. Define an algorithm for generating the abbreviation of any given name (string of letters).

4.20. An inventory control system is to be designed which will review the stock status of each article in the inventory daily. If the availability (stock on hand and reordered or recommended for reordering) of an article is below the reorder point for that article, the system should generate a replenishment recommendation. Normally, these recommendations will be held within the system until the weekly reorder summary is printed. Only if the availability of the article falls below a lower critical level is an urgent recommendation to be printed immediately. When the recommendations have been manually reviewed and a replenishment order placed (possibly for a different quantity), a message to this effect will be entered into the system.

In order to avoid confusion, the system should not normally print a second replenishment recommendation until manual action has been taken upon the first one. However, if an urgent recommendation has been printed in a daily run, later included in a weekly summary and still no order placed, then the system may issue a second recommendation if the criterion is met again. If no order is placed within a certain time after a recommendation first appeared on a weekly summary, the system should assume that the recommendation has been overlooked, cancel the recommendation, issue a warning notice to that effect and continue normally (usually issuing another recommendation for a different quantity). But such a recommendation should only be cancelled if it last appeared on a weekly summary, not on a daily list of urgent recommendations.

An urgent recommendation should be printed only once, of course. The weekly summary should include all open recommendations, whether printed previously or not.

Specify the logic for controlling the issuing and printing of recommendations in this application software system.

4.21. Consider the following modules written in COBOL:

Main program:
```
PROCEDURE DIVISION.
PARA.
   DISPLAY "MAIN PROGRAM" ERASE.
   CALL "MODA".
   CALL "MODB".
   CALL "MODA".
EXITPARA.
   STOP RUN.
```

MODA:
```
WORKING STORAGE SECTION.
01   DATA-A PIC X VALUE "1".
PROCEDURE DIVISION.
PARA.
```

```
        DISPLAY DATA-A.
        MOVE "2" TO DATA-A.
    EXITPARA.
        EXIT PROGRAM.

MODB:
    PROCEDURE DIVISION.
    PARA.
        DISPLAY "MODULE B".
    EXITPARA.
        EXIT PROGRAM.
```

What will be displayed on the video screen when the main program is executed? Why? Does it make any difference if the program's modules are overlaid or not?

Is the variable DATA-A in MODA a local or an own variable?

Concurrent execution of computational tasks

5.1. Consider a system for processing airline seat reservations in which seats for any particular flight may be reserved from any terminal. In particular, the system permits any number of terminals to reserve seats on the same flight essentially simultaneously. To enable this to be done, a computational task is established for each active terminal; data on any flight's reservation status is accessible by any computational task (i.e. is in a common data environment). Intermediate variables used by a particular computational task are assigned to that task's local data environment. The following is an extract of the algorithm proposed for reserving seats in this system:

        flight ← flight identification input from keyboard
        seatsdesired ← number input from keyboard
        IF seatsdesired ≤ available(flight)
        THEN available(flight) ← available(flight) − seatsdesired
        ELSE display message that seats are not available

where the array available is in the common data environment and all other variables referenced above are in the task's local data environment.

Would you expect any problems to arise during the operation of this system? If not, prove that the algorithm is correct. Otherwise, indicate the problems you would expect to arise. How can they be prevented?

5.2. Give an example of a deadlock in a system permitting concurrent execution of tasks.

5.3. How can a deadlock be prevented? Discuss in detail.

Computer arithmetic

6.1. In mathematics, the set of real numbers and the binary operations addition and multiplication form a field. Is the corresponding system of floating point arithmetic as implemented in a typical computer a field? Discuss in detail.

6.2. A particular computer system evaluates the expression $65000 - 65000 + .01 - .01$ and obtains the correct answer 0. When it evaluates the expression $65000 + .01 - 65000 - .01$, it obtains the obviously incorrect answer 0.0017175. Explain.

Computational complexity

7.1. What is meant by the computational complexity of an algorithm?

7.2. What is the time complexity of the following algorithm for searching a sequenced list for a given item?

```
linearsearch(key, start, end, searchkey);
FOR i ← start TO end STEP 1
IF key(i) = searchkey
THEN return the value of i as the value of linearsearch;
NEXT i
return the value of start − 1 as the value of linearsearch
```

7.3. What is the time complexity of the following algorithm for searching a sequenced list for a given item?

```
binarysearch(key, start, end, searchkey);
il ← start
ih ← end
WHILE il ≤ ih
DO BEGIN
    ip ← integer((il + ih)/2)
```

IF key(ip) < searchkey THEN il ← ip + 1
ELSE IF key(ip) > searchkey THEN ih ← ip − 1
ELSE return the value of ip as the value of binarysearch;
END;
return the value of start − 1 as the value of binarysearch

7.4. Interpret your answers to the above questions with regard to a situation in which a fast computer executes the linear search algorithm and a slow computer executes the binary search.
7.5. What is the maximum number of entries which can be stored in the stack when executing the non-recursive algorithm for quicksort (see question 4.13)?

Data structure

8.1. What is a sequential file?
8.2. What is a relative file?
8.3. What is an index?
8.4. What is an indexed file?
8.5. What is an inverted file?
8.6. What is a hierarchical index?
8.7. Why are indices sometimes structured hierarchically?

Program structure

9.1. What is meant by the terms modular programming, structured programming and hierarchical programming?
9.2. What are the advantages claimed for modular programming, structured programming and hierarchical programming?
9.3. When applying these programming techniques, how large should the designer make each single module?
9.4. What information must the specification and documentation of a single module contain?

Testing

10.1. What is the purpose of testing computer software?
10.2. What is "black-box" testing?

10.3. What is "white-box" testing?

10.4. How can the correctness of a module be demonstrated by black-box testing?

10.5. How can the correctness of a module be demonstrated by white-box testing?

10.6. What criteria should one use to decide when to stop testing a module or a system?

Project management

11.1. A project manager is in charge of a group of five programmers, each of whom will design and write between one and four closely related programs. All programs are part of one application system, for which general system specifications exist. The time required by each programmer to complete his own programs has been estimated; the estimates vary between six and eight months.

The project manager intends to monitor progress as follows. Every two weeks, each programmer is to report the percentage of his assigned work already completed and the number of hours actually worked on this project during the two week period. From this data, the project manager will calculate the number of hours each programmer still needs to complete his programs. Similarly, the projected completion date will be recalculated. The project manager will also use the data on hours worked to verify that the programmers are not spending more than the agreed amount of time on other projects.

How effective is this method of project management in your opinion?

11.2. Would you suggest any improvements to this method of project management?

11.3. What should a project manager do if the plan he has prepared calls for a much later completion date than is desired?

In closing

12.1. How would you describe the relevance of the material covered in this test to the detailed specification, design and development of computer software?

    a. quite relevant, but patchy in coverage, just scratches the surface
       of the applicable theoretical background
    b. relevant, but too mathematical, qualitative aspects neglected
    c. moderately relevant, but methods for selecting and using specific
       techniques, packages, etc. missing
    d. not very relevant, too theoretical, importance of the structure of
       the computer industry and of the strengths and weaknesses of
       the various sources of software and software personnel over-
       looked
    e. quite useless and irrelevant. Finding and hiring warm bodies
       who can spell computer programming without making too
       many mistakes is all that counts.

Postscript

It is suggested that the reader compare his answers with those in the
Mocpendium at the end of this book (see page 133 ff.) – even his answers
to those questions with which he had little or no difficulty. In some cases,
he may find that the answers in the Mocpendium give a different view of
the problem and its solution.

The typical reader will have had little difficulty with questions in some
areas, but will find that other questions covered unfamiliar topics. All
areas covered in this test are, as mentioned earlier, important to the
software practitioner. The reader who found certain areas difficult or
unfamiliar should, therefore, strive to complement his knowledge accordingly. The mature, professional software engineer must have a certain
command of all of the areas of knowledge covered in this test.

The reader who was able to answer essentially all the questions on this
test completely, correctly and with little difficulty may consider himself
to be an advanced software universalist. We need more of his kind in
software engineering. Such a reader should strive to transfer his breadth
of knowledge to others in the software field and to motivate others to
seek out such knowledge on their own.

Chapter 4

The practice of software design
and development: tomorrow?

The dangers of knowledge are not to be compared with the dangers of ignorance. Man is more likely to miss his way in darkness than in twilight; in twilight than in full sun.

Richard Whately (1787–1863)

The nature of the software world of the future will be determined by many factors, the most important of which are our own choices and decisions regarding what sort of a future we desire. We can have just about any kind of software future we want – provided that we are willing to make the appropriate decisions, to put forth the requisite effort and to take the necessary steps.

It is not the intention of this book to predict what our software future will be like, but rather to identify the alternatives open to us. It is up to the reader to weigh the advantages, disadvantages and costs of each alternative and to decide for himself which of the possible software futures he wants to strive to achieve.

The spectrum of possible software worlds of the future can be characterized by three extremes, called Future A, Future B and Future C in the paragraphs below. Any possible software future is intermediate to these three extremes. In the audacious Future A, much is attempted, capabilities are limited and major failures are frequent. In the backward Future B, strong pressures are present to restrict computer applications to those within the limited capabilities of the software practitioners and their customers. These systems are usually successfully realized, but of

course much is left undone. In the celestial Future C, the competence of
the average practitioner has been developed to such a high level that even
very complex applications are normally implemented without major
difficulty or problems of a fundamental nature. The extreme Future A
can be simply described as a reckless future; Future B, reactionary; and
Future C, radical.

The two dimensions of the space of possible software futures are the
average level of professional competence achieved by software practitioners (cf. the *how* issues, chapter 1) and the complexity of the applications attempted (cf. the *what* issues, chapter 1). The collapse rate is
determined by these two variables. The space of possible software futures
is represented below as a triangle with the Futures A, B and C at its
vertices:

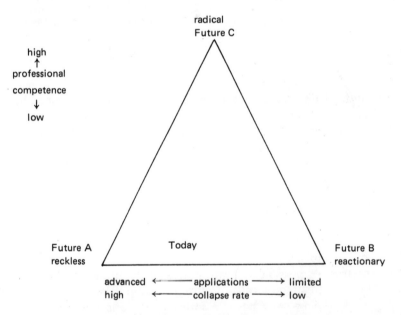

The characteristics of today's software world as discussed in chapter 2
place us between Future A and Future B, but closer to Future A. Many
trends and developments in data processing, especially the advent of the
microcomputer, will result in considerable pressure to apply computer
technology much more extensively throughout society in the next decades

[Evans]. This will push us even closer to the point representing Future A. If we decide to develop our professional software capability much more extensively in the future, we can deflect our path away from Future A and toward Future C. If we do not decide to do so, the catastrophic collapses characteristic of Future A can be expected to give rise to a wave of public reaction leading us to Future B.

In order that we may decide where in the triangle of future software worlds we want to position ourselves, let us look at each of the characteristic extremes – Future A, Future B and Future C – in more detail.

The reckless, audacious Future A

Future A represents the logical extension of our current world of software collapses. As computers are applied to a greater variety of tasks, involving human lives and public safety to an ever increasing extent, the consequences of software collapses will take on more and more frightening dimensions. Characteristic of the audacious Future A is that little restraint is exercised on what is attempted, completely inadequate efforts are made to acquire the necessary technical expertise and, as a result, major failures and catastrophes are common. In Future A, the software industry has become, in effect, an overly optimistic, blundering bull in a china shop.

Particularly applicable to Future A is what might be called the software corollary to Parkinson's Law and the Peter Principle: Software developers will conceive and try to build ever more complicated systems until the limit of their ability to cope with complexity is exceeded.

Despite our numerous past and present software collapses, there is today among broad segments of society an almost snug feeling of optimism and confidence in our computer based future. This state reminds one of the world situation in the eighteenth and early nineteenth centuries: continuous improvement and progress on all fronts seemed assured. In the world of science, for example, physics had attained a highly refined state by the middle of the nineteenth century; we knew and understood just about all there was to know and understand. Our knowledge was perfect, only a little minor polishing up remained to be done. Then, in the late nineteenth and early twentieth centuries, the bubble burst with unexpected, widespread and by no means only positive consequences. Social and political upheaval of a previously unimagined magnitude occurred. In the world of science, it became evident that old, cherished physical theories were hopelssly inadequate for describing a wide range of important phenomena and that a completely revised view of our physical world was required. A comparable shock could be awaiting us in the computer scene. There is a very real danger that we will allow our current euphoria to sweep us very close to the reckless, audacious Future A – where the reality bears little or no resemblance to our optimistic expectations.

If the audacious Future A comes to be, software situations something like those described below can be expected to occur. These episodes represent an extrapolation of the events of the past and present (see chapter 2). While entirely plausible, the episodes described below are, today, fiction. But how long will they remain fiction?

The quick descent

Four jumbo jets collided over Paris one cloudy morning. All 1,631 passengers and crew members as well as 525 people on the ground were killed. Another 1,000 people on the ground were injured. The damage to property was considerable. Traffic congestion, the worst ever recorded in the area, remained a major problem for two days. During this time only a small fraction of the area's 25,000 office workers could get to and from work.

The cause of the accident was identified as an obscure error in one section of the software used in the air traffic control system: if four airplanes were located in the second quadrant, if they were flying in a northeasterly direction (a flight pattern used only during unusual weather conditions) and if no airplane was in any other quadrant, a routine was executed in which a minus sign had been inadvertently omitted from one statement. This had the effect of bringing the airplanes together instead of directing them apart. The computerized air traffic control system had been in successful operation for over 20 months when the accident occurred.

Microprocessors and macrofires

One night, an unoccupied warehouse caught fire and burned to the ground. Investigators determined that the heating system had overheated an interior room in which inflammable chemicals were stored. At first, it was suspected that an arsonist had disabled the thermostatic controls, leaving the heating system turned on.

Further investigation revealed that similar fires had occurred in three other buildings in the preceding year. In all of these buildings a new, microprocessor controlled heating and air conditioning system had been installed. It was discovered that the software for this system contained a shortcoming or limitation which, however, could not clearly be classified as a mistake. When the temperature exceeded 128 degrees F., truncation of high order bits of the temperature variable in the program occurred. The program then "thought" that the room was much too cold instead of too hot, so it caused the room to be heated at the maximum possible rate. When the temperature reached the flash point of the inflammable material, the fire broke out.

The bigger they are, the harder they fall.

After an extended period of financial difficulty, one of the largest companies in a medium sized European country went into bankruptcy. Although lengthy investigations revealed many specific instances of errors, inconsistencies and delays in many management reports and operational documents, only vague and nebulous conclusions regarding the overall reasons for the failure of the company could be drawn. Only one thing was really clear: the company's information and communications systems were in such a state that the company had become unmanageable.

An old-fashioned Mocsian collapse

A thirty story building collapsed during construction. The building's designers, registered architects and civil engineers with many years of successful practice, conducted a detailed examination of the design and of the events leading to the accident. They discovered errors in the calculations of stresses in certain elements of the building's structure. Originally, all these calculations had been made and checked by computer.

The automated autobahn

Two months after a new automatic vehicle control system was installed in a section of an autobahn, an accident involving 400 automobiles occurred. It was determined that under certain conditions of traffic volume and velocity, the computer programs did not execute sufficiently fast. This, in turn, caused certain logical deficiencies in the program to affect the behaviour of the system which, in the specific case investigated, led to loss of control and to the collision.

Blackout at high noon

At noon one day, a computer controlled electrical power generating network shut itself off. The cause of the failure was found to be a combination of factors, one of which was a mistake in a computer program. The day before, two new power generators had been connected to the network, bringing the number of such stations to 257. Within the computer programs, the generator identification had previously been stored in an 8-bit field, so it had been necessary to modify the software in order to expand the size of this field. In the process, an obscure error was introduced into the program which caused one of the generators to be shut down at noon. This resulted in an overload being placed on the other generators, which were, in turn, shut down to protect them from damage.

A computer system can push the button.

The computerized defense control system of country A detected the initial phase of an enemy attack and placed its defense forces into full retaliatory status. A number of weapons were launched in accordance with country A's DECAP (defensive counterattack plan). Shortly after two of the nuclear missiles had been armed in flight, it was discovered that an error had been made; country A was not under attack after all.

The head of state of country A communicated with the leader of country B via their "hot line". Country A's leader apologized profusely, of course, for the erroneous counterattack against country B and solicited the latter's assistance in avoiding a catastrophe. Country B's defense system was able to intercept one of the two armed missiles, but the other one reached and destroyed its target: a military base and a neighboring town. Approximately 75,000 persons were killed; radioactivity effectively prevented access to the area for over a year.

The cause of the error was found to be a mistake in a computer program in the EAVES (enemy attack verification subsystem).

A computer controlled nuclear reactor

A major accident in a new nuclear reactor facility was caused by two software errors and a defective safety valve. The core overheated, the coolant boiled and part of the piping was burst by the excessive pressure. A large quantity of water containing radioactive contaminants was released into the central building, preventing access to the area for several months.

Analysis showed that the computer programs used to calculate heating rates within the reactor and the required cooling capacity contained a mistake. As a result, the cooling mechanisms in the core had been underdimensioned. When the reactor was first operated at full power, the core overheated slightly but not dangerously. As a result of a mistake in the reactor's operational control program, the rate of cooling, instead of the reactor's activity level, was reduced. This, of course, made matters worse instead of better and led finally to the damage to the reactor.

Management of the company operating the reactor pointed out that only in combination did the two mistakes in the software and the defective safety valve lead to the conditions which caused the accident.

An on-line, remotely accessed data base for medical diagnosis

Because a data base network system was inoperative for an entire weekend, a patient died. The doctors in attendance at the hospital to which he was taken were unable to diagnose the disease. As it turned out, the patient had contracted a relatively rare tropical disease while on a business trip. He first developed symptoms after returning home, where the disease was unknown among practicing physicians.

In the complex legal litigation which ensued, it was clearly shown that had the physicians been able to access the diagnostic data base, they would have been able to diagnose the unusual disease correctly and to prescribe appropriate therapy. The prognosis for the patient would then have been very good.

After the physicians were thereby absolved of responsibility for the patient's death, the controversy centered on the cause of the mistake in the software which resulted in the system's becoming inoperative. The system's developers were accused of professional incompetence on the grounds that they were not familiar with any of the professional (as opposed to the trade) literature on the design of data base and data communications software. They countered by claiming that the literature in question was of a highly theoretical nature and was, therefore, of no practical value. Their adversary's attorneys succeeded in demonstrating in court that the literature in question was of no value to the system's designers for another reason: they lacked the prerequisite knowledge for understanding it.

Furthermore, responsible members of the software supplier's management were accused of criminal neglect for having knowingly assigned unqualified personnel to the task of designing a system upon which human life would depend. Some even felt that they should be charged with being accessories to manslaughter.

Would you bank with a computer?

Because of mistakes in its software, an important system for clearing interbank transactions failed one Thursday morning. It was not discovered until Thursday afternoon, however, that transactions were being processed incorrectly. Finally, around noon on Friday, after feverish, all night activity, programmers succeeded in identifying the mistakes in the software. By Sunday evening, the software had been corrected, in time for the opening of business on Monday.

The conduct of the nation's business was severely disrupted, of course, by the banking system's long period of inoperation. During the early part of the week following the near catastrophe, the system was heavily overloaded with delayed transactions. Several weeks passed before most erroneously processed transactions were identified and corrected.

Fly away

A space vehicle with four astronauts on board was lost in deep space because of a mistake in a program in its navigational guidance system.

The vehicle was in the vicinity of the asteroid belt when its rockets were suddenly fired at full thrust, placing it on an incorrect course. By the time the error was discovered and a correction prepared for transmission to the computer on board the vehicle, it was beyond communication range. Calculations showed that it had gone into a highly eccentric orbit around the sun with a period of 203.554963 years. When the incident occurred, enough oxygen and provisions were on board to last the four astronauts approximately 10 months.

The annual survey on collapses

A major firm providing computer consultancy and market research services conducted an annual survey on failures of software development projects. A large sample of projects completed or abandoned during the preceding year was selected and analyzed in detail. Only projects involving more than 10 man years of effort were included.

The results of the survey indicated that the collapse rate had been slowly but steadily increasing for years. The last year's collapse rate was reported to be 62.4%. Another 19.7% of the projects included in the sample exhibited major shortcomings and problems but were judged to be salvageable.

The 2000 phenomenon

In the last weeks of the year 1999 and in early 2000, business in the computerized economies of the world all but collapsed. For bills rendered in 1999 but due in 2000, overdue notices were issued already in 1999, charging the debtor interest for some 99 years. After January 1, 2000, many systems failed to issue overdue notices for amounts due in 1999 but not yet paid. The data in many reports were printed in the incorrect sequence; data pertaining to the year 2000 preceded data for the year 1999 instead of following it. Many computer runs terminated abnormally during this time because of overflow and similar errors. For software maintenance personnel this was a very difficult and trying time, during which the time pressure under which they worked was unusually severe.

The problems could all be attributed to the widespread use of a two-digit field for the year in computerized data files. In the late 1970's, the 1980's and the early 1990's, programmers had made incorrect assumptions regarding the operational lifetimes of the programs and the data files they designed.

Epilogue to Future A

The underlying cause of the catastrophic collapses typical of Future A seems clear: computer applications were attempted which exceeded the effective capability of the available software designers and developers. Society has two basic options open for improving such a situation. It can 1) restrict what is attempted to that which is safely within the current reach of software practitioners (by modifying its position on the *what* issues) or it can 2) take action which will result in a fundamental and major increase in the abilities of its software designers and developers (by modifying its position on the *how* issues).

When incidents with consequences as serious as those outlined above begin to occur with sufficient frequency, a public reaction can be expected. It will consist of calls – some rational, some emotional – for legal and political action. The result will be some combination of 1) restricting and curtailing new developments based on computer technology and 2) social, political, legal and economic pressure to improve the quality of software products and the capabilities of software producers. Public reactions of these types have already occurred in connection with other engineering fields – most recently, for example, nuclear reactors for electrical power generation and proposed nuclear fuel reprocessing plants have been the targets of demonstrations and legal actions by groups of citizens in a number of countries.

If and when society decides that Future A is not acceptable and if reactions of the first type outlined above dominate, society's position on the *what* issues will change and a transition toward the reactionary Future B can be expected. If, instead, reactions of the second type outlined above prevail, society's position on the *how* issues will change and a transition toward the radical Future C will follow.

The reactionary, backward Future B

Characteristic of the reactionary Future B is that decisions on *what* issues are strongly and unduly influenced by the inappropriate and inadequate resolution of *how* issues. These very different types of issues become confused in the minds of lay citizens, who perceive computer technology itself (as opposed to its inept application) to be dangerous. To protect themselves, they then react in such a way as to restrict severely the application of the technology perceived to be so dangerous. The applications which are permitted are burdened by extensive and costly procedures for testing and verifying their safety and by a heavy legal liability. A low rate of occurrence of catastrophic failures is achieved, but at high cost in terms of monetary expense, long delays in realizing new applications and, probably most importantly, foregone benefits.

A situation similar in some respects (but less extreme) can be observed today in connection with nuclear technology. In the late 1940's and the 1950's, it was much touted as a means for achieving many benefits for mankind and as the key to a future world of plenty. In the 1960's and 1970's, as serious potential dangers were perceived by the public, this euphoria gave way to an antinuclear movement which in major countries succeeded in bringing nuclear reactor construction to a standstill for some time. If something similar happens in connection with computer technology, we might find ourselves in Future B.

If the backward Future B comes to be, software related situations something like the – currently – fictitious ones described below will occur.

Computers may not guide airplanes.

In a large country with a highly developed civil aviation industry, a law was passed to restrict the implementation of computerized air traffic control systems. The new law required very extensive testing of any new proposed system, including complete, parallel operation of the old and the new systems for an extended period of time. Only after 10 months of error free operation had been logged was the air traffic control agency allowed to convert to the new system.

In addition, the agency was required to take out public liability insurance in the amount of the equivalent of U.S.$ 10,000,000,000 if a computer system were used for automatically routing flights (as opposed to simply preparing data for display to human controllers). After the law was passed, a spokesman for one of the control centers announced that a new computer based system, fully developed and ready for implementation, would be scrapped. He explained that the cost of compliance with the new law would render the new system completely uneconomical.

The new law had been passed with little controversy after several major disasters, attributable primarily to mistakes in software, had occurred over a period of time. Public reaction to the disasters as well as the complex legal issues that had arisen in the various suits and counter-suits filed in the aftermath of the catastrophes led political leaders to conclude that drastic legislative measures were required.

Microprocessors and macrofires

A court of appeals upheld the ruling of a lower court which had decided that a supplier can, under certain conditions, be held liable for consequential damages resulting from errors in software embedded in a microprocessor based product. The case involved a microprocessor based control system for a heating and air conditioning installation. Errors in the system's control program had resulted in a large fire which caused personal injury and property damage.

The defendant in the case, a company supplying heating and air conditioning equipment, announced that this decision would force it to redesign a considerable number of its products. The new products, based on a more traditional technology, would be more expensive but less effective and less reliable. As a result, sales were expected to decline. The company would, in all likelihood, be forced later to lay off a significant fraction of its 2,500 employees.

Software collapses and job security

During lengthy negotiations, a union in a European country success-fully blocked the planned implementation of an extensive computer based information system in an organization which was one of the country's larger employers. When interviewed, the union's representative explained its position: "If the system would work as projected, substan-tial benefits could be expected. Management was willing to share these benefits with employees in ways which were acceptable to us. But if the system were to fail, a severe financial crisis would be the almost certain result. This would endanger the organization's existence and therefore, the jobs of a large number of employees. The risk was simply greater than we could responsibly accept."

Do not enter a building designed by computer.

During the course of designing a large building, a dispute arose between some of the architects and engineers involved. At a late stage of the project, some of them claimed that they had discovered errors in computer programs used to perform various design calculations. They insisted on redoing all calculations manually. They pointed out that it would be irresponsible to trust the computer calculations and proceed with construction as originally scheduled. Others felt that such a drastic step was unnecessary and much too costly. It was decided to proceed with the project without delay.

When the building was completed, the designers who had discovered the presence of the errors in the programs picketed the building. Of the people who came to the building during the first two weeks it was open, only about 10% actually entered it.

Ban the Computer.

When members of the interest group "Ban the Computer" discovered that applied research was being conducted on a computerized vehicle guidance and control system for automobile highways, they organized a massive reaction. Members and sympathizers staged a two day "sit in and lie in" strike on all major roads within some 50 km of the headquarters of a company which was partially funding the project. Threats of violence were directed at the project's chief scientists and engineers.

When plans for implementing an improved, computer based system for monitoring and controlling a large nuclear reactor were disclosed, combined anticomputer and antinuclear demonstrations were organized and conducted. The implementation of the system was delayed so long by demonstrations and by legal actions brought by "Ban the Computer" in local courts that the operator of the reactor finally discontinued the project.

A computer cannot be permitted to push the button.

The organization "International Friends of Peace" staged simultaneous, week long demonstrations in seven countries which maintained large and powerful military forces. These demonstrations were directed against the rumored forthcoming implementation of top secret computer based defense control systems which could automatically initiate a defensive counterattack. The outspoken president of the International Friends of Peace wrote in a press release, "It is bad enough that our political leaders, in a moment of irrationality, emotionality and/or lunacy can willfully decide to start W.N.W. I (World Nuclear War I). We cannot, and will not, allow our collective safety to be further endangered by a bug infested computer system understood by no one which can decide, against all our desires, to push the button."

As a result of the public reaction triggered by the demonstrations, the defense ministries of four of the countries announced that they would review their decision to participate in the international project to implement the system.

Don't wire me into your information society.

A new national service was offered which enabled a private individual, from a video terminal in his home, to access a variety of data collections offered by a number of organizations, to order merchandise from any one of a number of suppliers, etc. The system was capable of largely eliminating the need for traditional postal services, newspapers, many magazines and some library services. The cost of using the system was sufficiently low that it was definitely competitive economically with the classical services it could potentially replace.

Despite the obvious advantages of using such a system, it was not a commercial success. At the end of the system's first year of operation, fewer than 1% of the households in a large region had subscribed to the service. The organization operating the system commissioned a study of the reasons for the poor acceptance of the system by the public. The results of the study were perhaps best summarized by one of the persons interviewed when he said, "A friend of mine who has a terminal demonstrated the service to me once. You have to be an electrical engineer or a computer scientist to use it and even then it doesn't work half the time. If that's what your information society is all about, don't wire me in."

They wouldn't bank with a computer.

When a group of depositors of a bank learned that their bank's computer system was connected to a national banking network which had been plagued by various minor problems, they founded the "Depositor's Initiative Action Group". By the end of their second week of activity, in which they distributed brochures to other depositors, held discussion meetings, etc., approximately 35% of the bank's depositors had closed their accounts.

The radical, celestial Future C

Characteristic of the radical Future C is that high demands are placed on applications of computer technology and that the capabilities of both software personnel and computer system users have been developed to the extent that such high demands can be successfully and reliably met. When currently unrealistic desires are expressed, they are easily identified as such; where appropriate, the software researchers and developers set about complementing their knowledge and capabilities so that they will be able to meet these desires in the future.

Seen from our viewpoint today, the radical Future C represents a pleasant and ideal situation, seemingly a dream world. While Future C is not easily and effortlessly achievable, neither is it out of reach in the middle to long term. If we choose, we can start very soon to move in its direction. Our rate of progress in that direction will depend only upon how earnestly we want to achieve that state of affairs and upon how much effort we are willing to expend to achieve it.

If the celestial Future C comes to be, software connected situations something like those described below will occur. These episodes, while plausible and in principle possible, are fiction today. If we take the necessary steps, perhaps one day they will be reality.

Remaining aloft

A near miss situation was reported by a computerized, fully automated air traffic control system which had operated uneventfully and error free since its installation several years earlier. Two aircraft were suddenly found by the system to be on a collision course, 45 seconds flying time apart. The emergency subsystem automatically took control and directed the airplanes apart. Shortly thereafter, the system displayed information on the situation and the corrective action taken to (human) air traffic monitors on the ground and to the flight monitor on board each airplane involved.

The system identified the cause of the emergency to be a traffic volume which exceeded its design specifications by 34%. It pointed out that it would not be able to prevent reliably a collision if the overload exceeded 65%.

Electronic postal services for the home

A postal project involving the installation of electronic postal connections to 100,000 offices and private residences was completed on time and within budget. The new equipment and software functioned as planned from the very outset. In the first year of operation, no interruption of service was reported.

This system enables a subscriber to access, from his home or office, any one of a number of services offering selective access to news reports, business and professional literature, information for consumers, library catalogs, encyclopedias, other works of reference and many other similar collections of information. The subscriber can also send a message to any other subscriber, for example, an order for merchandise, a credit transfer to his bank, a bill to a customer, etc. He receives messages from other subscribers, for example, his bank statements, order confirmations, letters from friends and relatives, bills, etc.

Ban manual control of dangerous processes.

Despite warnings from a computerized control system for a nuclear reactor, an accident occurred. No one was injured. The only damage was to the reactor, which was out of service for six weeks for repair.

The incident was initiated by an operator's error. The computerized control system detected the error and warned the operator. Two successive actions recommended by the system were overridden by the operator. The system was finally compelled to take over control from the operator and shut down the reactor.

In a subsequent hearing, the operator stated that the chain of events took place so fast that a human was incapable of making rational, considered decisions effectively. Following the hearing, both public and expert opinion called for revising safety regulations to require more fully automated control of such processes. All agreed that a computerized control mechanism is better able to make critical decisions based on a great variety of data and in a fraction of a second than is a human operator.

Some things cannot be done – yet.

The director of the translation services division of an international, intergovernmental organization needed improved computer support for the rapidly growing activities of his division. He asked the computer support division for assistance in planning a new system which would accept voice input in any one of ten languages and spoken by any one of several hundred different people. The system was to provide translated output in the form of simulated speech, printed documents or microfilm.

Several experts in the fields of computer technology, linguistics and modern languages were assembled. After a short investigation, they reported that the current state of the art was not sufficiently advanced to permit the design and development of such a system intended for productive operation. While research was relatively advanced and promising in almost all areas relevant to the design of such a system, there were some small gaps in the spectrum of prerequisite knowledge and capabilities which effectively precluded the construction at that time of a properly engineered, effective and reliable system of the type needed.

No plans for pursuing the matter further were formulated at that time. It was recommended that the idea be reviewed again two years later.

No computer systems, no profit

A medium sized company, one of the oldest in existence in its field, became insolvent and went out of business. The company's demise was attributed to a variety of detailed causes, but all could be traced ultimately to outdated, mostly manually based systems and procedures used in the conduct the company's business. For example, fewer than a third of the company's managers and only about half of its clerical staff had convenient and direct access to the company's rather limited information systems. Few had any significant computer based support for their individual tasks. The company had not taken optimum advantage of modern devices and systems for increasing the productivity and the effectiveness of management and administrative staff. As a result, its cost structure and its inability to adapt quickly to changing market conditions rendered it unable to compete successfully against other, better equipped firms.

Relations between the company's management and union representatives had been strained for some time because, in the union's view, management took such a conservative and backward approach to the application of advanced information systems in the firm. Relations never broke down completely, however, because the more discontented employees resigned on their own initiative more or less continually during the several years preceding the insolvency. They invariably left to find more interesting and challenging work with other firms, where they could gain more valuable experience.

The "Softwaremation" annual survey

In the July, 2000, issue of the trade magazine "Softwaremation", it was reported in the annual feature article "Survey of the Software World" that the "fraction of system development effort devoted to testing and debugging declined this year to approximately 10% for medium and large systems. Most of the errors found during testing and debugging were of a typographical nature or were minor oversights which were quickly and easily corrected. Old-timers will recall (but newcomers will probably not believe) that some twenty years ago, this figure was well over 50%. The absolute amount of effort devoted to testing and debugging a typical system declined even more sharply, however, for overall productivity has improved (and hence total developmental effort for a particular system has declined) by a factor of 5 to 10 in the last two decades."

In another part of the survey, it was reported that "of a sample of 2,500 software development projects involving more than 5 man years of effort each, 60% were completed within the original time and cost budgets. Only 10% were completed more than 1 month late or at a cost exceeding 115% of the budget. (Almost all of these projects were at the forefront of the state of the art.) Slightly more than 98% of the projects met their specifications and were considered successful. On the negative side, three of the 2,500 projects were reported to be complete failures."

The survey also revealed that "practicing software developers are now more highly educated and professionally trained than ever before. Beyond the usual secondary education, the average coding technician has successfully completed a three year technical training program, including 6 months of industrial practice. The typical semi-professional software designer has completed a four year university level course, while every software engineer has completed a university level program of study lasting five years or longer. The average semi-professional designer and software engineer who graduated more than five years ago reported attending, during the past five years, professional development seminars totalling 20 weeks in length.

"Of the coding technicians included in the survey, 30% regularly read professional papers available through the various on-line professional literature services, while 83% of the semi-professional designers and 100% of the software engineers reported doing so."

Chapter 5

The path from today to tomorrow

> *We see it is accounted an error to commit a
> natural body to empiric physicians, which
> commonly have a few pleasing receipts
> whereupon they are confident and adventur-
> ous, but know neither the cause of diseases,
> nor the complexions of patients, nor peril of
> accidents, nor the true method of cures: we
> see it is a like error to rely upon advocates
> or lawyers, which are only men of practice
> and not grounded in their books, who are
> many times easily surprised when matter
> falleth out besides their experience, to the
> prejudice of the causes they handle.*
>
> *Francis Bacon (1561–1626)*
>
> *Ignorance is the curse of God; knowledge
> the wing wherewith we fly to heaven.*
>
> *William Shakespeare (1564–1616)*

How can we proceed to a better software world of the future? First, we
must agree that we do, in fact, have a serious problem which must be
solved. Because a great deal of software is being produced and because
the net benefits derived from our computer systems are so great, some
might be inclined to conclude that we don't *really* have a problem at all.

Chapter 2 examined what is wrong with the current software situation.
It is evident that there is a considerable and growing gap between supply
and demand for software, that we are incurring unnecessarily high costs
and inconvenience in developing and using software today and that the
potential danger to the public of software failures is increasing. I.e., both

105

the quantity and the quality of our software fall far short of satisfying our needs and the shortfall is, if anything, increasing.

If we do conclude that we have serious and fundamental problems which should be corrected, then we must decide whether we want a better software future earnestly enough to take active steps to change the direction in which we are currently going. We must decide whether we are willing to expend the extra effort required to achieve that better software future.

The path of least resistance: the passive approach

We will decide whether and how to improve our method of software production. If that decision is made by default, that is, if we make no conscious decision but simply continue to muddle along more or less as we are now doing, the future is relatively clear. The very impressive improvements in microelectronics and computer hardware will support an increasing – even accelerating – demand for many more new, advanced applications of computer technology. Already many futurologists are predicting the advent of wondrous, advanced applications affecting large segments of society in the rather near future (see e.g. [Evans]).

The advanced applications referred to above are, in most cases, clearly within the grasp of our current technology – in principle. But where are all the highly qualified software designers and developers to come from who will be needed to make these systems? Our quantitatively and qualitatively limited capability to design and develop software will restrict severely what we will be able to accomplish *in practice* in the foreseeable future. While it is clear that the potential demand for software will increase substantially, it is not at all clear that the supply will increase correspondingly, the hopes and beliefs of some futurologists notwithstanding [Evans, p. 238]. Even if more people can be applied to software development, it is not clear that sheer quantity can substitute for missing quality. Seldom, if ever, can brute force compensate for a lack of professional skill, ability and competence.

Unless a very major and fundamental improvement is made in our ability to design and develop complex software in quantity, the strong demand for advanced applications will lead us to attempt software systems which will, in many cases, be well beyond the capabilities of the software practitioners assigned to their development. The demand for increasing numbers of software systems will induce greater numbers of underqualified people to join the ranks of software developers. As a result of these two tendencies, one can expect software productivity to stagnate or even to decline, the collapse rate to increase and the consequences of software failures to become more severe and serious. In short, we will move in the direction of the reckless, audacious Future A described in chapter 4.

When serious incidents of the types characteristic of Future A (see chapter 4) begin to occur with sufficient frequency, a public reaction will result. It will consist of calls – some rational, some emotional – for legal and political action. As discussed in chapter 4, the result will be some combination of 1) restricting the application of computer technology and 2) pressure to improve the quality of software products and the capabilities of software producers. As long as we follow a comparatively passive approach, the response to the pressure of the second type (the improvements in software capabilities) will be less than satisfactory and the pressure of the first type (to restrict new applications) will dominate. This pressure will then push us in the direction of the reactionary, backward Future B.

An unexpectedly sluggish acceptance or a curtailment of new developments based on computer technology could have a serious negative effect on the world economy, for computer technology represents perhaps the most promising basis for future growth and improvement in the industrialized countries. But if its exploitation by inadequately prepared technicians brings more cost, danger, damage and risk than benefit to society, that exploitation must – and will – be restricted.

Some of the various types of pressure to improve the quality of our software products and the capabilities of our software producers can also be expected to have a restrictive effect on new applications of computer technology. The introduction of legal liability for damages resulting from the effects of software errors would force software suppliers to take the correctness of their products more seriously. This would presumably lead them to employ only those programmers capable of producing correspondingly reliable software. The registration and/or licensing of software engineers, at least of those working on certain types of critical systems, will be proposed more frequently and will certainly be considered more seriously in the future. If the supply of appropriately qualified software practitioners is not increased substantially, software output will be restricted.

More direct pressure from users of software systems can also be expected. Today, such pressure usually takes a relatively mild and passive form: the user department by-passes the EDP department when procuring systems to solve its problems, for example. In the future, we can expect disgruntled management of the user departments to convince upper management that it is time to put as much pressure on the EDP manager as is necessary to get him to put his house in order. The turnover rate of EDP managers will, in all likelihood, increase somewhat as a result, but this will not bring about an overall improvement in the software development area. On the contrary, a conservative reaction can be expected.

Industry will continue its search for more and better tools and techniques for designing and developing software. At the same time, the call for more practically oriented training of more software practitioners will continue.

Marginal improvements will continue to be made in all these areas, but the potential demand for software will grow even more rapidly. The result will be a large and growing backlog of desired but unrealized software systems, continuing increase in the number of unqualified entrants into the field of software production, at best a marginal improvement in software quality and increased frustration and disappointment on the part of all involved. In short, we will have more of everything – good and bad.

The old saying "the road to hell is paved with good intentions" applies to the path resulting from the passive approach. While one might argue about whether the reckless Future A – the first station on that path – or the reactionary Future B – the end of that path – is hell, it is clear that neither is heaven. Neither of these is the sort of future in fashion among technological prophets today.

Good intentions are not enough if a better software future is to be achieved. If we want to move in the direction of the radical Future C, we must be willing to put forth considerable and intelligently guided effort, taking an active, instead of a passive, approach.

The path to ideal results: the active approach

The situation outlined above can be avoided – but only if we want a better software future seriously enough to take active steps to change the direction in which we are currently going.

Probably the most important change which must be made is to "get down to basics". Just as the finest surgical instrument is of value only when in the hands of a professionally trained and skilled surgeon, so are the tools and techniques of our software technology of full value only when applied by professionally trained and skilled software engineers. Much more emphasis must be placed on building the necessary base of fundamental knowledge among a much larger fraction of our software producing practitioners. Much less emphasis should be placed on the search for magical, panacean tools and techniques.

If one traces the productive ancestry of any software system – through the programming department, software house or computer manufacturer which supplied it, through all the compilers, assemblers, program generators, editors, other tools and techniques used to develop it, etc. – ultimately the human brain will be found to be its original progenitor. The human brain is, therefore, the primary factor of production of software. A software system can be only as good as its developers' intellects are capable of making it. The quality of a software system depends directly upon the extent to which the intellects creating it have been developed to synthesize logically consistent structures of considerable complexity.

To improve the quality of our software, the quality of the intellects which produce it must, therefore, be improved. To increase our quantitative capacity to create software, the requisite knowledge and skills must be transferred to a greater number of human minds. In other words, to improve the quality of our software, better education must be provided for our software practitioners; to increase our productive capacity, more practitioners must be educated. Providing more and better tools and techniques to practitioners inadequately equipped intellectually to employ them creatively will not solve our software problems any more than producing more and sharper scalpels or equipping more operating rooms will advance our medical profession's ability and capacity to transplant organs successfully.

Educating software practitioners does not mean having them memorize the syntactical rules of some particular programming language or the various technical idiosyncracies of some particular system or systems; such "knowledge" is no more adequate a background for designing and developing software systems than the ability to hold a scalpel and make a straight incision is an adequate preparation for performing surgery. Such skills are necessary, but far from sufficient, conditions for success in the respective fields of endeavor.

When considering the educational needs resulting from the application of computer software technology, it is useful to consider generally the educational paths followed by those persons technically responsible for the application of older technologies to society's various needs. The designers and developers of buildings of all types, bridges, production plants of all types, electrical equipment of all kinds (including computers and communication equipment), nuclear reactors, ships, automobiles, aircraft, space vehicles, medicines and other chemical preparations, etc. must all have completed a several year, academically oriented, university level course of instruction before practicing their professions. While this was not always so, society has, in the course of the last century or so, found such an educational background highly desirable as a preparation for these occupations – and in many cases, necessary as a means of protecting itself from the consequences of mistakes perpetrated by mountebanks and charlatans.

Society found that it was schizophrenic to believe that an educational system adequate for a relatively decentralized, non-industrialized, rural society with only loose economic coupling between its various parts could suffice for a society in which the application of relatively advanced technologies had become an important aspect of economic life. With technological advance came the need for a correspondingly more intense educational preparation both of the technical specialists and, to a somewhat lesser extent, of the population as a whole. And as our society continues to become increasingly dependent upon the ever more extensive application of newer, more advanced technologies, so does the need for education increase still further. If this increased need for education is not satisfied, further technological development will be inhibited. Both the fraction of the population which receives a higher level education and the average length of such education must continue to increase, for it is illusory to think that only a secondary education is an adequate preparation for a creative role in the highly technological world and complex society of today and tomorrow. One component of this general trend is the need for a much more extensive educational preparation of our software designers.

On the other hand, society has found by experience that less thoroughly trained persons – technicians, mechanics, etc. – can in most cases be employed to construct, install, operate and repair the above mentioned technological products (although construction is usually monitored by professionals). But in the case of software, these activities involve relatively less effort (and therefore should presumably require relatively fewer people to perform them) than is the case with other engineering fields. The construction phase for software systems is relatively insignificant, for even writing the last few lines of program code involves making design decisions. Repairing (as opposed to correcting errors in the design or modifying the design) is all but unknown in software systems, being confined to reloading a correct copy of software altered by hardware malfunction or by errors in other parts of the software. (Software, in contrast to physical objects, does not wear or otherwise change its characteristics as a result of use and hence never needs repair in the traditional sense of the word.)

The following examples illustrate why an academic education is useful – even necessary – for designers of the types of technological products mentioned above. Without a working knowledge of calculus, it is difficult, if not impossible, to really understand why an electrical circuit containing inductance, capacitance and resistance resonates, under what conditions it is underdamped, critically damped or overdamped and why the factor $2*pi$ occurs in the formula for the resonant frequency. Without knowledge of calculus and of Maxwell's equations describing the physical behaviour of electromagnetic fields, the electrical technician will have difficulty understanding why a transmission line has a characteristic impedance and what the significance of this property is. With a working knowledge of calculus and the relevant areas of physics, the electrical engineer can derive the corresponding formulae and analyze the behaviour of such circuits and transmission lines relatively easily. (Anyone who uses a telephone should be glad that some electrical engineer took such phenomena correctly into account when the telephone equipment and network he uses was designed. If the engineer had not, echoes, oscillation, resonance, inadequate frequency response and many other effects would make communication impossible.) Similarly, the building technician will not be able to calculate stresses and strains in beams loaded and supported in ways not described in his designers' handbook. He can memorize or look up formulae and apply them to situations already encountered and solved by someone else, but he cannot work out solutions to new problems involving unusual configurations of loads and supporting restraints. The mechanical or civil engineer, with his knowledge of the relevant areas of mathematics, will be able to solve the differential equation describing the bending of a beam with new and unusual boundary conditions in order to determine the stresses which the beam will have to withstand. And perhaps more importantly, if he does not have the mathematical knowledge he needs to solve his problem, he will recognize that fact and will be able to turn to the mathematical literature to acquire the needed knowledge.

The same types of considerations apply to the design and development of computer software. Many programmers are – often without realizing it – somewhat hamstrung by the lack of recursive facilities in the programming languages they use. Many programmers still write slow internal sorting routines because they have never read about "quicksort", even though it appeared in the professional literature almost two decades ago. Many have programmed a particular function the long, hard way, not realizing that by applying a little knowledge of finite automata, they could reduce the complexity of their task quite considerably. Many a software designer has specified erroneous logic because he was not able to simplify a boolean expression correctly. Still today some file management systems are being developed which implement indexed files in such a way that overflow areas and attendant, rather harsh restrictions are forced upon the application programmer and the user – even though simple and more effective solutions to the problems involved can be found in the professional literature (and in some operational systems as well). It still occurs that only after a software system is completely developed do its designers discover that it executes unacceptably slowly when the quantity of input data is large. When its designers do not know how to calculate the time complexity of the algorithm used (perhaps because they do not even know what time complexity is), they are not able to determine such behavioural characteristics of their products earlier and at less expense.

Noteworthy is the absence of software from the above list of technological products whose designers are expected today to be professionally educated. As we have seen in chapter 2, professional educational programs exist for software engineers, but only a very small minority of our software designers and developers has had the opportunity to complete such courses. Thus it is evident that, among all technologically based fields, we are handling the education of the majority of our software designers and developers in a truly unique way today. It is not, however, at all evident that there is a rational justification, based in the nature of software technology, for this unique approach to the education and training of its practitioners. On the contrary, this state of affairs is almost certainly due in the final analysis only to the relative newness of the field. Sooner or later, we will find it necessary to educate software designers and developers in fundamentally the same manner as we educate designers and developers in other technologically based fields. Until we do, the software field will not be able to fulfill is obligations to society properly and responsibly. Until we do, we will not make significant progress toward Future C.

Where must we begin if we are to make our way toward Future C? Who must do what to bring about a real improvement? All concerned with the design and development of software – including the users – must take some action. Without concerted efforts by all parties, no really significant improvement can be expected. Some attitudes must be changed, particularly notions of what is a socially and economically acceptable modus operandi. We must become more demanding with respect to the reliability and quality of our software. Users must become more discriminating and less willing to accept software products of low quality. Management of software development groups must become more discriminating and less willing to employ underqualified personnel and must take more effective steps to improve their employees' fundamental knowledge and basic skills in software development. Educational leaders and educators must work to improve very greatly the quantity, quality and effectiveness of programs for developing software practitioners. Software practitioners must work, individually and collectively, to improve substantially their own knowledge of relevant subjects and must become more aware of the limits of their knowledge. Other members of society must recognize the need for improvement and must demand, encourage and actively support the corresponding efforts of those directly involved. Finally, all must deemphasize somewhat short term objectives and benefits in exchange for more substantial improvements in the medium to long term – that is, everyone must be willing to demand and produce relatively less software for use today in order to invest in our ability to produce more and better software tomorrow. If we fail to make such an investment today, tomorrow's software will be – at best – only marginally better and only slightly more plentiful than today's and the celestial Future C will be nothing more than an elusive dream.

Communication in the software development process

The process of software development consists of transforming the user's perception of his problem into machine language program code which will execute on a computer in such a way as to assist the user in solving his problem. This process necessarily involves translating the user's perception of his problem through several stages of specifications, algorithms and computer programs. A number of intermediaries must communicate with each other in order to complete this process successfully. These intermediaries form a communication chain beginning with the user, passing usually through a user oriented information analyst, the computer oriented system analyst, the programmer (in the narrow sense of the term, i.e. the coder) and a multitude of software aids (editors, generators, compilers, loaders, file management systems, utilities, the operating system, etc.).

The following diagram illustrates the intermediaries and their communication overlaps in a typical and reasonably successful software development project today:

Problem   Machine

        User

            User analyst

                    System analyst

                            Programmer

                                    System software

Notice that only adjacent intermediaries in the communication and translation chain are really able to communicate effectively with one another. Usually (as in the above illustration) the areas of knowledge of, for example, the user oriented analyst and the programmer do not overlap enough to enable these people to communicate with one another effectively. Even if they could communicate, their areas of interest and concern do not overlap either, so there is little motivation for them to communicate.

In such a situation, the entire chain of communication is totally dependent upon each intermediary. If any one makes mistakes in his part of the process of translating the problem into a program, there is a good chance that no one else will detect the error until the system has been completed and found to be unsatisfactory in some respect.

All too frequently, the communication overlaps in the design process are more accurately illustrated by the following diagram:

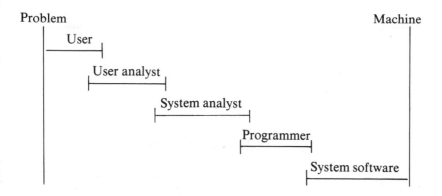

Here, the areas of overlap are so small that even adjacent intermediaries in the chain are barely able to communicate. Many misunderstandings and oversights will result. Probably the final software system will be of poor quality, if it is usable at all. The probability that it will satisfy the user's real needs is low.

The system analyst's primary task is not to analyze, but rather, of course, to synthesize a system. Recognizing this, "system analyst" is replaced by the more accurate and descriptive term "system designer" in the following discussion. Furthermore, all persons referred to above are involved directly in the process of specifying, defining and preparing computer programs and are therefore programmers in a broad sense of the word. Reflecting this, the job title "programmer" above is changed to "coding technician" below. With regard to the tasks typically performed by the "system analyst" and by the "programmer", the distinction between "designer" and "technician" is more appropriate, accurate and important than the currently made distinction between "system" and "program" – a distinction based on the rather arbitrary and solely technical difference between one program and a collection of related programs (i.e., a system).

In order to progress toward the radical Future C, the effectiveness of communication in the design process must be improved by, among other things, increasing the overlap of the knowledge and of the areas of concern between the various parties involved. Ideally, it should become possible for non-adjacent intermediaries to understand and to communicate with each other, at least to some extent:

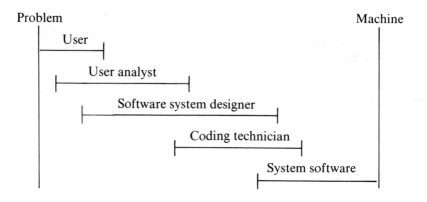

Being in the middle of the communication and translation chain, the system designer is here able to communicate with more intermediaries than anyone else – in fact, he is the only one able to communicate with every other intermediary. He thus assumes what is probably the most critical role in the entire design process. If he has a software engineering background, he should have a broader understanding of the system software than the coding technician does (even though the latter works directly with it more frequently). In this case, the diagram becomes:

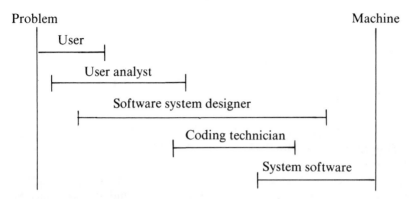

While the absolute range of knowledge and skill required by each person is greater in the situation represented by this last diagram than in the current situations represented by the first two diagrams above, the relative role of the coding technician has been reduced in importance. He is being "squeezed out", so to speak, by the somewhat more extensive capabilities of the system software on the one side and by the significantly increased scope of the system designer's responsibilities and abilities on the other. In this last diagram, the coding technician has become a sort of skilled assistant to the designer. His task is to translate into detailed program code the algorithms and data structures previously specified and defined by the designer. The coding technician performs his work under the supervision of the designer, just as a technician in any other field performs his work today under the supervision of the engineer responsible for the design of the product being developed.

In order to minimize development costs, one might be tempted to eliminate the user analyst in the above diagram. Unless the communication overlap between the user and the system designer is extensive, one should resist this temptation. Yielding to it and eliminating the user analyst could reintroduce a weak link in the communication chain, increasing again the likelihood of inadequate communication and, therefore, of mistakes and inadequacies in the final system.

The guarantee duality

One of the main differences between the professional and the non-professional supplier of goods or services relates to what they guarantee.

The professional never guarantees results, he guarantees instead a certain level of personal qualification for performing the service offered. For example, the physician does not guarantee that his patient will recover, but he does guarantee that his medical knowledge and occupational skills meet specified minimum requirements. The lawyer does not guarantee that he will win his client's case in court, but rather that he has sufficient knowledge and skill to handle the case in a proper way. The architect does not legally guarantee that his client will find the house or building he designs to be ideal in any particular way, but rather that he possesses the necessary qualifications to be able to design a structure which will meet the applicable building codes and which will not collapse as long as environmental conditions remain within accepted design norms for the area. Similarly, the engineer does not guarantee per se that his design will fulfill a particular need, but rather that his knowledge and his ability to apply it are adequate to design the structure or product to meet the specified criteria under the specified conditions – or to be able to recognize that the state of the art does not permit the specified criteria to be met reliably. By implication, the professional's qualifications will ensure that the services rendered will, in general, satisfy accepted, overall standards of quality, but no guarantee of success is made in any particular case. Any legal claim against the professional must be based in the final analysis upon his lack of (or substandard) qualifications or upon his carelessness or negligence in applying his knowledge or skill, not upon his failure per se to deliver services of any particular level of quality in any specific situation.

In the case of the non-professional, the situation is precisely reversed. He does not make any formal representation regarding his personal qualifications or abilities; instead, he guarantees that the services rendered (or goods delivered) will satisfy previously agreed standards or specifications. If, in any particular case, the goods or his services prove unsatisfactory, he must make amends. His qualifications or lack thereof are irrelevant with regard to a dispute over the adequacy of his goods or services.

Today, software is in a no man's land. The disclaimer still frequently found attached to software products states that the supplier makes no warranties regarding the correctness, suitability or quality of the software provided. But neither does he make any formal representations regarding his qualifications to design and develop the software in question. This seems patently unfair to the purchaser, who clearly has a right to demand some sort of guarantee of the quality of the goods or services he obtains. The reasons for this situation are, on the other hand, obvious and perfectly understandable: The typical software designer does not possess relevant qualifications of a professional level and hence cannot guarantee them. Furthermore, he realizes that he is not capable of designing and developing a complex software system in which he can have enough confidence that he can guarantee its performance. I.e., the inability to guarantee anything in connection with software is due in both instances to the inadequate qualification of the typical software designer today.

If reasonable progress is to be made in the direction of Future C, the qualifications of software practitioners must be improved so that they can guarantee something rather than nothing. It would seem to be most appropriate to take the professional approach for projects involving design work near the forefront of the state of the art – i.e., guarantee the qualifications of the designers but not the design itself. For design work of a more routine nature, well within the state of the art and not representing a significant departure from existing designs, the non-professional route could be taken – i.e. guarantee the design itself, not the professional qualifications of its designers. Today and in the foreseeable future, a large fraction of our software design and development work is likely to fall into the first category, for which the professional approach would seem to be the more appropriate one.

Who must do what?

If progress is to be made toward the radical, celestial Future C, everyone directly concerned with designing and developing software as well as everyone involved in their education and training must take active steps to improve the current software situation. Included among these are software users and their managers who today all too often make critical decisions on the basis of an incomplete – sometimes even faulty – understanding of the issues and alternatives.

In the paragraphs below, general suggestions for the steps to be taken by each of the following groups are given:

– members of the academic community,

- managers of software development groups,
- software practitioners (today's "system analysts" and "programmers"),
- software users and user management and
- educators in the secondary schools.

The academician

Of the many areas in which special effort is required in order to progress toward Future C, perhaps the most extensive changes must be made within the academic community. In particular, its capacity in the software oriented areas of computer science must be increased very significantly. Academicians should pay more attention to the middle and long term needs of industry but, if anything, less attention to its short term needs than is now the case. The teaching of programming language X and operating system Y on computer system Z should not receive high priority in a computer science or software engineering curriculum simply because the university happens to have those systems installed or because a faculty member is familiar with them. Instead, the fundamental properties of data, data structures and algorithms, the structure, syntax and semantics of programming languages, "comparative programming linguistics", the organization of computational structures and mechanisms, the functions and structure of operating systems, the principles of operation of computing systems, etc., should be emphasized.

It is essential that those areas of mathematics which are relevant to these topics be given a high priority in the software engineering curriculum. Many fundamental ideas in information processing are actually quite old and well known – under different names – in mathematics. The terms used by the software practitioner often tend to disguise this fact. (The software practitioner talks of commands, instructions, operations, reformatting; the mathematician talks of functions, operators, mappings. The software practitioner talks of data, data elements, data types, data values; the mathematician talks of variables, sets, elements of sets.) If they manage to communicate, the mathematician recognizes – in mathematical terms – what the software practitioner is talking about; but all too often the software practitioner fails to recognize what the mathematician is talking about, even when it is quite relevant to computing.

If all this is done, the new software engineering graduate will have the background knowledge he needs to understand quickly and thoroughly a new system with which he will be confronted five or ten years later. Especially in a field changing as rapidly as computer technology, the initial educational preparation of practitioners must place greater emphasis on fundamental knowledge which is not subject to obsolescence and less emphasis on technical details which will be of little value in a few years and which tend to narrow, rather than broaden, the practitioner's mental horizons.

While close cooperation between academia and industry is called for in order to expose students to real problems, the students' exposure to real solutions must be handled with great care. Many real solutions provide good examples of how not to do things. Many others are not pedagogically useful as examples at all. Too few are good examples of the right way to do things.

Also important in the software engineering curriculum are courses in the fields of application for which the student plans to design and develop software during his career. Finally, his professional courses should cover business economics, project management and organizational structure and behaviour.

The underlying goal of the education of software engineers (or of any other academic education, for that matter) should be to prepare the graduate to learn on his own throughout the rest of his working life. He should learn how to seek and acquire new knowledge later as the need for it arises, when his professors are no longer available to assist him. He should, at the end of his formal education, understand the languages (technical, mathematical as well as natural) in which the professional literature of later interest to him will be written.

If this goal is not met, then the graduate cannot be considered to be a properly educated software engineer; he will have received only a technical training adequate for the first few years of a career as a better coding technician. The aim of the academic education of the software engineer should be to prepare him for his entire career, not to train him for his first two or three years on the job. Educators have the responsibility to reduce or eliminate the causes of software problems in the medium term future; solving current problems is a task which must be left largely to others.

The software development manager

Throughout the software producing sector of society the software development manager should strive to eliminate the current distinction between "system analysts" and "programmers" (coders), a distinction based on the technical definition of "a program". Instead, one should distinguish between professionally qualified designers of data and algorithmic structures (regardless of whether these structures are contained entirely within one program or whether they extend over many programs) on the one hand and coding technicians on the other hand. The qualifications and skills required by the practitioner as well as the value of his contribution depend primarily on the nature of the task (creative design vs. routine coding), not on the size of the structure designed or developed.

Through his hiring and training policies, the software development manager should strive to develop a relatively greater number of designers and a relatively smaller number of coding technicians in the future. With the better programming languages, the step between the specification of the algorithm and the program code is often not so great that someone is needed only for writing the code. In many cases, the skilled designer will need less time to produce the code for a particular algorithm than to communicate the requirements to the coding technician, review the resulting code and assist him in finding and correcting mistakes. To an increasing extent, the skilled designer is likely to find it advantageous to use an ad hoc program generator or already existing skeleton programs to produce large quantities of similarly structured code. Employment, training and educational policies should be formulated to anticipate this shift in needs rather than to react to it after developing the wrong mix of people.

The manager of a group of software practitioners must strive to increase the level of knowledge and skill of the members of his group. One way to do this is to set higher standards for new employees. Another, perhaps more difficult to achieve, is to upgrade the capabilities of his present employees by setting goals for improvement and by assisting them in meeting those goals, for example by arranging appropriate training programs, internal professional development seminars, etc. Such training must be of an on-going nature if it is to be effective; little will be accomplished by conducting on-again, off-again crash programs in response to individual crises.

In order to offset the mistakes of the past, these programs should emphasize fundamentals (see "The academician" above). Among the more basic and fundamental topics in computer science, the methodology for proving the correctness of programs is perhaps a particularly appropriate subject for training programs for practitioners. Teaching it can convey an increased appreciation for and understanding of fundamental principles. At the same time, it is directly applicable to practical problems and attacks head on one of our most pressing problems: software fraught with errors. In addition, software development personnel should be encouraged to increase their communication overlap with users (see "Communication in the software development process" on page 114).

By putting continued effort into such training, the manager will be able to increase his subordinates' knowledge of fundamentals significantly. Slowly, but surely, his programmers' productivity and the quality of their software will improve noticeably. If he is able to restrain his understandable desire for immediate, cosmetic results, he may succeed in avoiding the pitfalls of a search for the magic techniques which do not exist.

In order to achieve and maintain a higher level of knowledge and skill among a group of software practitioners, it is essential that they be given convenient access to the relevant professional literature. While every EDP department has shelves full of manuals on the specific software systems in use on its computers, few, if any, have books, journals, etc. on relevant computer science subjects in their libraries. (An investment of $1,000 or so in a good selection of such books and professional journals can often bring surprisingly large benefits in a short time.) Even fewer software development managers provide their personnel with access to any of the many on-line professional literature indexing services.

Organizations must be prepared to adjust the formal and informal status of their software designers and developers if they are to attract and hold more highly qualified personnel. While employers must expect to pay higher salaries to better qualified personnel, they can expect in return more than correspondingly higher productivity and software quality – provided, of course, that they know how and are organized to utilize the better qualified programmers. The difference in productivity among individual software practitioners is so great that the productivity of a software development group is much more dependent upon the quality than upon the quantity of its personnel. Cheap quantity can never substitute for expensive quality – if several well qualified software developers have difficulty developing a particular system, one can be certain that a much larger number of "three week wonders" will have even greater difficulty with it – if they are able to complete the system at all.

Clear distinctions in status, responsibility, authority and pay must be introduced between professionally qualified designers and less thoroughly trained and experienced coding technicians – just as such distinctions are drawn in engineering laboratories between engineers and technicians. Difficulties can be expected, especially during the transitional period and when new and old programmers of significantly different levels of ability and qualification are working side by side. Such difficulties must be brought out into the open and resolved, however, not avoided or brushed under the carpet.

One must avoid the temptation to utilize a good coding technician as a designer when he does not possess the requisite knowledge and skill. Neither the coding technician nor the user of the software will be served by doing so.

Most small and many medium sized EDP departments in user companies would be well advised to consider seriously whether they should attempt to develop new software systems or whether they should in the future contract with organizations of professionally qualified software engineers for this work. Such an EDP department may not have a sufficient variety of developmental work to provide the atmosphere and experience necessary to attract and to maintain sufficiently qualified personnel. System developers in such companies run a serious risk of becoming technically obsolescent in a few years. All too often, one finds that instead of getting five years of experience in five years they get one year of experience five times. They are frequently exposed to only one EDP philosophy and to only one computer system (both of which can easily become outdated over a period of not so many years). As a group, they tend to become "inbred" and after a few years often exhibit corresponding weaknesses. The alternative, bringing in "fresh blood" frequently, often leads to an undesirable amount of disruption and discontinuity.

By setting higher and more selective standards for new programmers, the software development manager can apply pressure both on new entrants to the software field to take full advantage of available educational programs and on educational institutions to prepare more thoroughly greater numbers of software engineers. If a software development manager is interviewing a "three week wonder" (or a candidate "three week wonder") for a programming position in a commercial organization, it is probably best for the manager to be frank with the applicant: The only thing the employer can really offer the applicant is a low level job as a coding technician with little real potential for advancement into a designer's position. In the long run, the applicant, the manager and society as a whole would all be better off if the prospective programmer were to get a proper educational preparation for a career in software development. As much as the manager would like to, he is simply not in a position to provide a new programmer with that background. Budgetary and commercial restraints prevent him from doing so.

The software development manager must consciously recognize that it is not possible to produce even medium sized software systems of only moderate complexity reliably and economically with inadequately qualified personnel. While software engineering differs in detail from other engineering disciplines, it is not inherently simpler. Therefore, software designers and developers are needed who are at least as well qualified in their field as are other engineers in theirs. Undertaking the development of software systems with underqualified personnel serves only to increase the software collapse rate still further and to hinder progress toward Future C. A software development project for which only underqualified personnel are available is better left unstarted.

The software practitioner

In order to start moving in the direction of the radical, celestial Future C, each programmer (again, in the broadest sense of the term) must strive to improve his own capabilities. While he can and should expect his employer to support his efforts toward self-improvement and to offer appropriate opportunities, each software practitioner must be prepared to take the initiative in this endeavour. He should not expect his employer to teach and train him; he should instead take it upon himself to search out and acquire additional knowledge of relevance. In his efforts to do so, he should let his own middle and long term personal interests influence his choice of topics for self-study. This will lead him to de-emphasize technical detail of temporary relevance and value and to concentrate instead on fundamental knowledge of a more general nature and of lasting relevance and value to his entire career.

The software practitioner should take steps to improve his ability to read the professional literature in order to gain easier and more effective access to this vast source of knowledge. He should also attempt to increase his "communication overlap" with others involved in the software development process (see "Communication in the software development process" on page 114). This he can do by learning more about the worlds in which they live and work, their problems, goals, objectives, etc.

When selecting an employer, the software practitioner should pay particular attention to the quality and value of the experience he will gain on the job offered to him. He should try to assess the professional qualifications of his prospective superior and of his prospective peers. He should consider carefully the policies of each prospective employer regarding professional development of the software staff and each prospective superior's willingness to support the employee's own efforts toward self-improvement. In particular, he should look for evidence of the employer's commitment to continuous (rather than sporadic) training of the software staff.

The software practitioner should attempt to discover the limits of his current knowledge. It is as important that he know what he doesn't know as it is that he have a broad range of specialized knowledge. The theoretical and professional computer science literature relevant to software engineering is extensive but not so much so that it is impossible to acquire a reasonably good overview of it. Only a moderate – but continual – effort is necessary to acquire and maintain an adequate awareness of what is available in that body of literature and knowledge.

Perhaps most importantly, the prospective new entrant to the field of software development should, before ever entering the job market, consider carefully whether he should obtain more formal education as a preparation for his intended career. A few years of immediate and good pay may be more tempting than a few years of additional, expensive study, but yielding to this temptation is a very shortsighted way to begin a working career which will last some 40 to 50 years. The current boom times for "three week wonders" may very well not last that long; the new entrant to the field of software development who implicitly assumes that they will is taking on a very great risk over the course of his working lifetime. Neither the individual nor society is served by basing such an important and final decision – whose various direct effects will last for about half a century – solely upon the monetary rewards to be received in the first few years only.

The software user

Purchasers and users of software can make a significant contribution to progress simply by becoming less willing to compromise on software quality – if necessary, by explicitly foregoing substandard systems today in favor of better ones tomorrow. Users should realize that cheap software is, in reality, either useless or quite expensive, frequently both. The costs of correcting and overcoming the effects of faults in the software can, over the lifetime of a system, greatly exceed the difference between the initial costs of the cheap and the good software. While purchasers should shop around for bargains of good quality, they must be prepared to face up to the distinct possibility that their hopes and expectations may be unrealistic.

Users and, in particular, user management must learn to recognize the difference between what one can in principle accomplish with computer support on the one hand and what a particular group of people can achieve in a particular organization within a limited period of time on the other hand. They must find the golden mean between euphoria over what is in principle possible and exaggerated pessimism resulting from negative experiences. They must come to realize that custom software of acceptable quality cannot be made cheaply or by underqualified personnel. They must recognize that standard software ("packages"), distributed to many users, may or may not satisfy their own particular needs – and that the burden of determining the suitability of such software rests squarely upon the user's shoulders.

While the user and his management should not and cannot expect to become computer experts, they should take active steps to increase significantly their familiarity with computer technology, its possibilities, its inherent limitations and our current limitations in applying it to practical needs. By doing so, they will put themselves into a better position to make effective, meaningful and realistic decisions regarding the application of computer technology to their particular needs. Also, they will increase their "communication overlap" with the software practitioners, thereby facilitating communication in the process of planning and implementing computer based systems (see "Communication in the software development process" on page 114).

The secondary school educator

Secondary schools must make major efforts to increase the quantity and improve the quality of their computer oriented instruction. Especially they must stress basic concepts and principles of informational processes in their curricula; any technical detail they teach is almost certain to be obsolescent by the time the pupil has the opportunity to apply such knowledge in practice. Secondary school teachers must avoid the temptation to teach watered-down versions of decade old courses in particular programming languages, using texts which have been modernized in style but not in content.

Undoubtedly the most difficult problem in this regard facing secondary school management is the severe shortage of teachers qualified to teach computing subjects. The teachers of history, languages, sciences, mathematics, etc., have all studied various aspects of their subjects for several years in college. The teacher of computer subjects who has taken two or three semesters of college courses in this field is comparatively well prepared; most of his contemporaries have had even less exposure to computing. This unsatisfactory situation must, of course, be remedied. In the short term, secondary school management will have to rely primarily on summer programs and self-study to improve their teachers' qualifications. They should encourage and support such activities more extensively than is usual in the case of other fields. In the longer term, they should set higher and more selective standards for newly hired teachers of computing subjects. In the meantime until these measures bear fruit, secondary schools should take advantage of whatever assistance they can obtain from local businesses and from their parent bodies, provided, of course, that adequate quality can be ensured.

Teachers of computing subjects in secondary schools should beware of a potential pitfall and take special care to avoid producing "compulsive programmers" [Weizenbaum, chapter 4]. The student who is obsessed with inconsequential and often trivial internal technical details of the computer system and who is almost neurotically detached from the realities of the world to which the computer is being applied is not likely to make significant contributions to society later in life. Teachers must strive to present computing subjects in such a way that the student develops a balanced appreciation for both computer technicalities and the requirements of the application. He should not be encouraged to become involved with the computer solely for its own sake, but rather should come to see it as a useful instrument for achieving other worthwhile goals.

It is difficult to overemphasize the importance of the way in which computing subjects are handled in secondary schools. Within a few decades – by the time pupils currently in secondary schools reach the middle of their working careers – a very large fraction of the population will almost certainly be in regular, direct contact with computer based systems of various types. The effectiveness with which people will be able to utilize these systems – even their willingness to use such systems at all – will depend to a significant extent on their early preparation and exposure to the possibilities of computer systems. The widespread application of any technology requires mutual adaptation of the technology and the society employing it. The ability and willingness of tomorrow's population to adapt this new technology to their needs and to adapt their social structure to the possibilities and constraints of computer technology depend in no small measure upon their early introduction to this technology.

Conclusions

Sooner or later, computer technology will play as important a role in our society and economy as do the automobile, electrical power, electronics, the telephone, the airplane, radio and television today – technologies upon which our way of life depends totally. The major restraint on its progress will be imposed by software, not hardware, factors. The rate of progress in applying computer technology to society's needs on a widespread basis will be determined by our success – or failure – in overcoming the serious software problems discussed earlier in this book. The country or countries which succeed first in finding truly satisfactory solutions to these problems will likely enjoy a significant competitive advantage in the economic world of tomorrow.

The successful and widespread application of each of the technologies mentioned in the above paragraph became possible only after a cadre of professionally trained engineers had come into existence. Only after the number of professionals in any one of these fields reached a certain threshold was it possible to apply the respective technology to the direct benefit of most members of society. Only then was society able to take optimum advantage of the possibilities offered by that technology.

The same applies to the software field. But in the case of software, the "take off point" has not yet been reached. Until an adequate number of sufficiently well qualified software engineers has been developed, society will not be able to utilize computer technology in as widespread and effective a way as it already utilizes the other technologies mentioned above. The sooner we develop these important resources, the sooner we will be able to enjoy the benefits of a properly and reliably functioning computer software industry.

Can a transition from the current state of software affairs to a properly developed engineering discipline be successfully achieved in practice? The effort required is considerable and, just as in Moc, there are a number of restraining forces. But all of the other technological fields mentioned above have successfully accomplished this transition in the past – under similarly difficult conditions. Given a decisive will to make the transition and a willingness to expend moderate effort, the chances for success are undoubtedly very good. But if the will is lacking or if those parties directly involved are too lazy or shortsighted to invest the required effort, the software situation can only become worse. In the

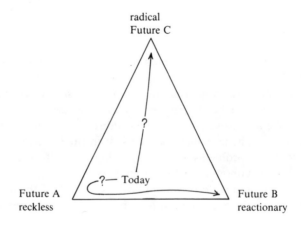

words of Edmund Burke (1729–1797), "The only thing necessary for the triumph of evil is for good men to do nothing."

In summary, everyone concerned with the unsatisfactory state of affairs in the software field today can and must do his part to improve the situation. Having created the problems over a period of at least two decades, one cannot realistically expect to solve them overnight. With conscious, concerted effort they can, however, be solved in the middle term – provided everyone starts now.

Omnipotent, panacean tools and techniques for the software designer and program coder do not exist. No tools, no techniques can compensate for the software practitioner's lack of knowledge, understanding and skill. The real cause of all software ills is the inadequate fundamental knowledge and understanding of informational processes among software designers and developers, not the lack of better tools and techniques. Until this shortcoming is corrected, the quality of our software will remain poor.

Mocpendium: Answers for practitioners of the science/art/craft/trade/racket of software design and development

Data and algorithms: basic concepts, definitions and axioms

1.1. A variable or a data element is an association of three entities: a name, a set and a particular element of that set. The particular element of the set is called the *value* of the variable.

Example: (X, integers, 43) is a variable named X which can take on (i.e., be associated with) integral values. The value of X is (currently) 43.

Example: (EMPLOYEE-IN-PERSONNEL-RECORD, alphanumeric strings 20 characters long, "Jones, John E.   ") is a variable named EMPLOYEE-IN-PERSONNEL-RECORD whose current value is "Jones, John E.   ". This variable takes on values selected from the set of sequences of letters and special characters exactly 20 characters long. The special characters (as well as the particular alphabet of letters to be used) must be precisely specified to complete the definition.

Example: (ADDRESS, alphanumeric strings at most 255 characters long, "") is a variable whose current value is the null string (a sequence of zero characters). Note that this variable can assume values of different lengths.

1.2. The *type* of a variable in essence characterizes the set of values which the variable may assume. The set may be defined explicitly (as above).

Often, expecially in older programming languages such as COBOL, the set is implicitly defined by describing the way in which a variable is to be represented in the computer's memory. For example, the picture phrase S9999 defines the value set as the set of all integers between −9999 and +9999, inclusive. The picture phrase 999 defines the value set as the set of all integers between 0 and 999 inclusive. See [Dahl, section II.2] and [Wirth, p. 4].

1.3. An array is a set of variables with similar names. The name of each subscripted variable in the array is of the form arrayname(i), where i (the subscript or index) is an element of a set I. I is usually a finite subset of the integers or the Cartesian product of a finite number of such subsets. (I.e., the subscript is usually an integer or an n-tuple of integers.) It is usual (but not, in principle, necessary) that all subscripted variables in one array be of the same type, that is, take on values in the same set. See [Wirth, section 1.6].

1.4. The word "algorithm" can be defined in rather general or in quite specific ways. In general, an algorithm is a precisely and unambiguously specified procedure for doing something, usually of a computational or information processing nature. For our purposes, an algorithm is best thought of as a sequence of statements. The statements in the algorithm are executed in an order determined by precise rules. The execution of each statement causes a precisely defined action to be performed. See [Knuth, Vol. 1, pp. 1–9], [Schnorr, chapter 1] and [Weizenbaum].

1.5. A data environment is a collection (set) of variables. It is generally useful to think of data on input/output devices as variables and to include these in the definition of a data environment.

If variable names are required to be unique within a particular data environment, then that data environment defines a mapping from a variable name into a value.

If different variables within a particular data environment are permitted to have the same name, then precise rules must be laid down for resolving naming conflicts.

1.6. A computational task is the association of an algorithm, a data environment and a processor (a mechanism for executing the algorithm).

The execution of the algorithm results in general in changes to the associated data environment.

1.7. A data declaration is a statement which defines an association between a variable name and a set of values. The declaration thus establishes the existence of the variable and defines its name and type. In some programming languages, a data declaration also serves to define an initial value of the variable.

1.8. An assignment statement defines or redefines (changes) the value of a variable, usually identified by name. Most commonly, the association between the variable name and a set of values has already been established when an assignment statement is executed (takes effect). If not, an implicit declaration statement is, in some programming languages, assumed before the assignment statement takes effect. See [Aho, p. 35], [Knuth, Vol. 1, p. 3] and [Manna, pp. 162–163].

Example: x ← 5 + y. Five is added to the current value of the variable whose name is y and the resulting number is assigned as the new value of the variable whose name is x.

1.9. A *global* variable is a variable which is defined at all times during the execution of a computational process.

A *local* variable is a variable which exists—i.e., is an element of the data environment—only while a certain task or a certain part of an algorithm is active (is executing). The variable is said to be *local* to the task or to that part of the algorithm. When the task is no longer active or when statements in the given part of the algorithm are not being executed, the variable does not exist (and is therefore not accessible).

An *own* variable is a variable which is global in existence but local in access. That is, only statements within the part of the algorithm "owning" the variable are allowed to access the variable (i.e. use its value or modify the variable in any way). The own variable continues to exist, however, when statements outside the given part of the algorithm are executing, even though such statements are not permitted to access the variable. Own variables are sometimes used within a subroutine which must "remember" what it did during a previous execution, such as a pseudo-random number generator, a module for reading sequential files, etc. See [Naur, 1962].

1.10. A conditional statement is a structure of the form:

IF condition THEN statement 1 ELSE statement 2

The condition is a logical expression (proposition) which can be evaluated to determine whether it is true or false. If the condition evaluates to "true", then the entire conditional statement above is equivalent to "statement 1". If the condition evaluates to "false", the entire conditional statement is equivalent to "statement 2". See [Aho, pp. 34–35] and [Manna, pp. 162–163].

Two statements are, by definition, equivalent when they have exactly the same meaning and, when executed, have exactly the same effect upon the data environment.

1.11. A WHILE statement is a statement of the form:

WHILE condition DO statement 1

When encountered in the process of executing an algorithm, the condition is evaluated. If the condition evaluates to "false", statement 1 is not executed; the execution of the algorithm proceeds with succeeding statements or as otherwise determined by the rules of hierarchically superior constructions. If the condition evaluates to "true", statement 1 is executed and the WHILE statement is executed again as described above.

In flow chart terminology, the WHILE statement is equivalent to the following:

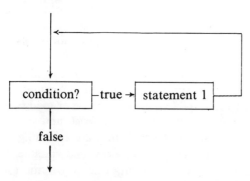

The WHILE statement is a fundamental construction for loop control in algorithms. Various other loop constructions appear in the many programming languages; almost all can be defined in terms of the WHILE statement. The reverse is not true, therefore the WHILE statement can be thought of as a sort of universal loop construction. See [Aho, pp. 34–35] and [McGowan, p. 20 ff.].

1.12. The FOR statement and loop

```
FOR var ← first TO last STEP incr
statement 1
NEXT var
```

can be defined to mean

```
var ← first
WHILE (incr ⩾ 0 AND first ⩽ var AND var ⩽ last)
    OR
        (incr < 0 AND first ⩾ var AND var ⩾ last)
DO {statement 1; var ← var + incr}
```

Note that in some computer systems the FOR statement has been implemented slightly differently. In some, statement 1 is always executed at least once. In others, implicit assignment statements are executed which assign the values of first, last and incr to internal variables before the loop is executed; in this case, only these internal variables are referenced when evaluating the loop condition. These different definitions of the FOR statement can, of course, lead to different behaviour during execution and often limit the extent to which a program written for one computing system can be run on another.

1.13. A linear list is a sequence of data elements or groups of related data elements. The only structural property of interest is the one-dimensional relationship expressed by positional adjacency in the sequence, hence the name *linear*. See [Knuth, Vol. 1, section 2.2].

1.14. A linked linear list is a linear list which is implemented in the following way. Each term in the sequence consists of a group of subscripted variables with the same subscript. The value of one of the subscripted variables, called the *pointer* variable, is the subscript of the next term in the sequence. A particular value of the pointer variable is reserved to indicate the end of the list. See [Knuth, Vol. 1, section 2.2.3].

1.15. A stack is a specific form of a linear list. Items are stored and
retrieved one at a time and only at one end of the list. Items are retrieved
in the reverse order in which they were stored (last in first out). See [Aho,
pp. 47–48].

1.16. A recursive algorithm is an algorithm which, during its execution,
invokes (calls upon) itself. Mathematical functions which are defined in
terms of themselves are often calculated by means of recursive algorithms. The following is an example of a recursive algorithm for calculating the factorial of a number:

```
FUNCTION factorial (n);
IF n = 0
THEN return 1 as the value of factorial
ELSE return the value of n * factorial (n − 1)
        as the value of factorial;
```

The following is an example of a recursive algorithm for summing the
values of the subscripted variables $x(1), x(2), \ldots, x(n)$:

```
FUNCTION sum(n);
IF n = 0
THEN return 0 as the value of sum
ELSE return the value of x(n) + sum (n − 1)
        as the value of sum;
```

See [Aho, section 2.3] and [McGowan, section 4.5].

Automata

2.1. A Turing machine is an abstract model for a computing device. It
consists of a tape with an unlimited number of cells, a read/write head
and a central control device which may be in any one of a finite number
of states. Depending upon the state of the control device and the symbol
in the cell currently under the head, the symbol in that cell may be
overwritten with a different one, the head moved one place to the left or
right and the state of the control device changed.

Using Turing machines, a number of important and fundamental
theorems have been proved about the "computability" of certain classes

of functions, the decidability of various classes of mathematical and logical questions and the equivalence of computing devices exhibiting different structures. See for example [Brady], [Manna] and [Weizenbaum].

2.2. A finite automaton (finite state machine) is another abstract model for a computing device. It receives an input stimulus and, depending upon its internal state, emits some particular response and undergoes a transition to another internal state. Mathematically, a finite automaton can be defined as a quintuple (In, Out, States, response, nextstate), where

In   is a set of input symbols,
Out   is a set of output symbols,
States   is a finite set of internal states,
response is a function on In∗States into Out and
nextstate is a function on In∗States into States.

Given an initial state and an input symbol, the functions response and nextstate define an element of Out (the output symbol) and an element of States (the next state) respectively. This state and another input symbol, in turn, define another output symbol and the next state, etc. In this way, a finite automaton provides a basis for defining a function on the set of sequences of elements of In into the set of sequences of elements of Out. Expressed differently, a finite automaton in effect maps an initial state and a string of input symbols into a string of output symbols.

It is sometimes convenient to define the range of the function response to be Out* (the set of all finite sequences of elements of Out) instead of the set Out.

A number of information processing tasks of practical importance can be solved quite simply, easily and efficiently by a straightforward application of this concept. In addition, finite automata are of theoretical interest. See [Arbib], [Brady], [Manna] and [Minsky].

2.3. An automaton A1 with initial state s1 and an automaton A2 with initial state s2 are said to be equivalent when they respond to any string of input symbols with the same string of output symbols.

It can be shown that two automata A1 = (In, Out, States 1, resp 1, next 1) and A2 = (In, Out, States 2, resp 2, next 2) starting in states s1 of States 1 and s2 of States 2 respectively are equivalent if there exists a function c on States 1 into States 2 such that

1. resp 1 (s, i) = resp 2 (c(s), i),
2. c (next 1 (s, i)) = next 2 (c(s), i) and
3. c (s1) = s2

for all s in States 1 and all i in In. The function c represents a correspondence between equivalent states of the two machines. Equation 1 above expresses the requirement that the two automata respond identically when in equivalent states. Equation 2 expresses the requirement that the two automata undergo transitions to equivalent states from equivalent states. Equation 3 expresses the requirement that the initial states be equivalent.

If the set c (States 1) contains fewer elements than States 1, then the function c reduces A1 to an equivalent machine with fewer states.

2.4. A von Neumann machine is another model for a computing device. Of tremendous impact on the world of practical computing and data processing, it has served as the basis for the design of the vast majority of the digital computers built since the late 1940's. It has a memory divided into cells, each of which may contain data or a part of the program. Depending upon the contents of the memory cell referenced by the program counter (a special register containing a number), the contents of one or more memory cells as well as the number stored in the program counter are altered in a precisely defined way. The process is then repeated indefinitely.

Abstract machines based on the structural principles underlying the von Neumann machine have been mathematically defined, for example, the RAM [Aho, section 1.2] and the RASP [Aho, section 1.4].

Boolean algebra

3.1. Boolean algebra, as applied to the design of computer hardware and software systems, is an algebraic system in which each variable may take on one of only two possible values. The two values are most commonly called "true" and "false" or "0" and "1". Three fundamental operations, AND, OR and NOT are defined.

In designing and coding computer software, the ability to manipulate

Boolean algebraic expressions is useful. The conditions in IF and WHILE statements (see the earlier questions on these statements) are, for example, expressions in Boolean algebra.

Mathematically, Boolean algebras are normally defined in a somewhat more general, axiomatic way. See [Harrison, chapter 2] and [Royden, chaper 15, section 2].

3.2. The AND function has two arguments and is defined as follows:

x	y	x AND y
false	false	false
false	true	false
true	false	false
true	true	true

This function is clearly commutative (x AND y = y AND x for all possible values of x and y). It is also associative, as can be seen from the following table:

x	y	z	x AND (y AND z)	(x AND y) AND z
false	false	false	false	false
false	false	true	false	false
false	true	false	false	false
false	true	true	false	false
true	false	false	false	false
true	false	true	false	false
true	true	false	false	false
true	true	true	true	true

Because the AND function is associative, we can write

   x AND y AND z

for x AND (y AND z) or for (x AND y) AND z without ambiguity.

3.3. The OR function has two arguments and is defined as follows:

x	y	x OR y
false	false	false
false	true	true
true	false	true
true	true	true

This function is clearly commutative. It is also associative.

3.4. The NOT function has only one argument and is defined as follows:

x	NOT x
false	true
true	false

Note that the NOT function is its own inverse, i.e. NOT (NOT x) = x for all possible values of x.

3.5. The two expressions are equal. Applying the above definitions of the functions AND, OR and NOT, we have:

x	y	NOT (x AND y)	(NOT x) OR (NOT y)
false	false	true	true
false	true	true	true
true	false	true	true
true	true	false	false

3.6. The two expressions are equal. To prove, construct a table as in the answer to the previous question.

Note the symmetry of the functions AND and OR with respect to negation (the NOT function):

NOT (x AND y) = (NOT x) OR (NOT y)
NOT (x OR y) = (NOT x) AND (NOT y)

Thus, each of the functions AND and OR can be expressed in terms of the other and the NOT function:

x AND y = NOT ((NOT x) OR (NOT y))
x OR y = NOT ((NOT x) AND (NOT y))

3.7. They are equivalent.

Proof: The condition (Boolean expression) x has only two possible values, true or false. Consider these two cases separately:

Case A: x = true.

By the definition of the IF statement, statement a is equivalent to statement 1.

By the definition of the NOT function, NOT x = false. By the definition of the IF statement, statement b is equivalent to statement 1. Statements a and b are both equivalent to statement 1 and hence to each other.

Case B: x = false.

By the definition of the IF statement, statement a is equivalent to statement 2.

By the definition of the NOT function, NOT x = true. By the definition of the IF statement, statement b is equivalent to statement 2. Statements a and b are both equivalent to statement 2 and hence to each other.

I.e., for every possible value of the condition x, statements a and b are equivalent. QED

In the above proof, we have assumed that two statements equivalent to the same statement are equivalent to each other. This follows from the definition of equivalence given in the answer to question 1.10.

3.8. By applying the results of the preceding question, statement a is equivalent to

IF NOT (x AND y) THEN statement 2 ELSE statement 1

But NOT (x AND y) = (NOT x) OR (NOT y). Substituting the latter expression for the former in the IF statement above, statement b is obtained. QED

3.9. The required Boolean expressions (conditional expressions) are:

a. (lastname (i) < lastname (j)) OR (lastname (i) =
   lastname (j) AND firstname (i) < firstname (j))
b. (lastname (i) > lastname (j)) OR (lastname (i) =
   lastname (j) AND firstname (i) > firstname (j))
c. lastname (i) = lastname (j) AND firstname (i) = firstname (j)

Note that each of the relational functions $\leqslant$, $\geqslant$, $<$ and $>$ maps a pair of values in a linearly ordered set to the set {true, false}. The relational function = maps a pair of values in any non-empty set to the set {true, false}. In the above expressions, the relational operators take precedence over the Boolean operators.

3.10. A simplified, equivalent statement is

IF x OR y THEN statement 1 ELSE statement 2

In the given IF statement, statement 2 is executed if and only if x is false and y is false, i.e. if and only if the expression (NOT x) AND (NOT y) is true. Otherwise, statement 1 is executed. The given IF statement is therefore equivalent to

IF (NOT x) AND (NOT y) THEN statement 2 ELSE statement 1

But (NOT x) AND (NOT y) = NOT (x OR y) (see exercise 3.6 above). Substituting this into the above IF statement, we obtain

IF NOT (x OR y) THEN statement 2 ELSE statement 1

which is equivalent to

IF x OR y THEN statement 1 ELSE statement 2

Algorithms: implementation, execution and correctness

4.1. Recursion is implemented by using a stack. Whenever a computational task is called (activated, invoked), all variables local to the calling task are stored in the stack. Among these local variables is control information indicating at what point in the calling task execution was suspended. When the called task terminates, its local variables are deleted from the data environment, the calling task's local variables are retrieved from the stack and execution of the calling task continues. The calling task may, in this scheme, activate another task using the same algorithm (program, subroutine, etc.) as it is itself using, i.e. the algorithm may be ·recursive. In general, such a mode of operation presupposes that the algorithm will not be modified during its use – in particular, that it does not modify itself.

4.2. Proposition: If n is a non-negative integer, the algorithm terminates with

$$\text{sum} = \sum_{j=1}^{n} x(j).$$

Proof: Consider the flow chart of the algorithm: '

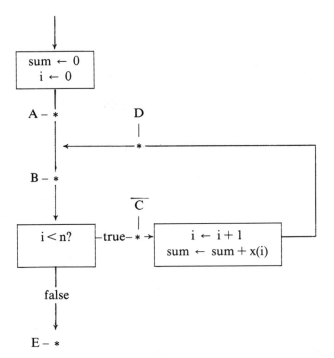

In this proof, we will show that a particular condition involving the values of the variables i and sum is always true at the points A, B, C, D and E in the flow chart above. Although the values of the variables i and sum are varying during the execution of the loop, the value of this condition does not vary. It is therefore called the *loop invariant*. The concept of the loop invariant is probably one of the most important ideas in designing and coding programs. It deserves to be much more widely known among programmers.

We will then use the fact that the loop invariant is true at all these points of the flow chart to show that the algorithm terminates with the stated value of sum.

The loop invariant is

$$\text{sum} = \sum_{j=1}^{i} x(j).$$

At point A, the variables i and sum both have the value 0, so the loop invariant is clearly true. The first time execution proceeds through points B and C, the loop invariant will also be true.

Let ic be the value of the variable i at point C and id be the value of i at point D. Similarly, let sumc be the value of the variable sum at point C and sumd be the value of sum at point D. We assume axiomatically that the execution of the two statements in the DO part of the WHILE statement has the effect that

$$id = ic + 1$$

and

$$sumd = sumc + x(id)$$

If the loop invariant is true at point C, then

$$sumc = \sum_{j=1}^{ic} x(j),$$

which implies that

$$
\begin{aligned}
sumd &= \sum_{j=1}^{ic} x(j) + x(ic + 1) \\
&= \sum_{j=1}^{ic+1} x(j) \\
&= \sum_{j=1}^{id} x(j),
\end{aligned}
$$

i.e., the loop invariant is also true at point D.

Since the loop invariant is true when execution passes through point C for the first time, it is also true when execution passes through point D for the first time. It will therefore be true the second time through points B, C, D, etc. Thus, the loop invariant will always be true at points A, B, C and D. If execution ever passes to point E, it will be true there, also.

A second condition is also invariant: $i \leqslant n$. (The reader should prove that this condition is true at points A, B, C, D and E.)

If execution passes to point E, i.e., if the algorithm terminates, we have the two conditions

$$\text{sum} = \sum_{j=1}^{i} x(j)$$

$i \leqslant n$

and the WHILE exit condition NOT $(i < n)$. Therefore, $i = n$ and

$$\text{sum} = \sum_{j=1}^{n} x(j).$$

We have proved that if the algorithm terminates, it yields the correct answer. Such an algorithm is called *partially correct*. To prove that the algorithm is *totally correct*, we must, in addition, prove that it terminates (in finite time).

To prove that the algorithm terminates, consider the sequence of values of i at point B as the loop is repeatedly executed. When execution passes through point B the first time, the value of i is 0. The second time, the value of i is 1; the third time, 2, etc. The value of i increases by 1 each time through the loop; as soon as $i \geqslant n$, the loop will terminate. Thus the algorithm will terminate after the statements in the DO part of the WHILE statement have been executed n (a finite number of) times. Assuming axiomatically that each statement in the loop executes in finite time, the loop will terminate in finite time. QED

Note the five key steps in the proof:
1. Identify the loop invariant.
2. Prove that the initialization of the loop establishes the truth of the loop invariant.
3. Prove that the body of the loop maintains the truth of the loop invariant.
4. Show that the loop invariant and the termination condition together imply that the calculated result is correct.
5. Prove that the loop terminates.

Notice also that we have made certain axiomatic assumptions about the effects of the execution of various types of statements on the data environment. In addition to those explicitly pointed out in the above proof, we have assumed that the evaluation of an IF or a WHILE condition has no effect on the data environment. One must be careful to verify that the system on which an algorithm is to be executed in fact fulfills all axioms required by its proof. If any such axioms are violated by the real system in question, then the proof clearly does not apply to the execution of the algorithm on that system.

The reader who is unfamiliar with correctness proofs should review the above proof until he understands all steps and how they fit together. This pattern forms the basis for the proof of the correctness of most loops in algorithms. The structure of this proof is particularly useful to the coder when he is writing his algorithm; often he can derive the algorithm from his outline of a proof of its correctness. A later exercise will illustrate this approach.

The reader will find more information on correctness proofs, verification of programs, ensuring program reliability and loop invariants in [Brady], [Kimm], [Manna] and [McGowan].

4.3. Proposition: If n is a non-negative integer, this algorithm terminates and returns the factorial of n as the value of the function, i.e. the algorithm is totally correct.

Proof: We will prove this proposition by induction on n. We begin by restating the mathematical definition of the factorial of a non-negative integer:

$$\text{factorial}(n) := \quad n * \text{factorial}(n-1), \quad \text{if } n > 0,$$
$$1, \qquad\qquad\qquad \text{otherwise.}$$

If $n = 0$, then the body of the algorithm is equivalent to "return 1 as the value of factorial". In this case, the algorithm is clearly totally correct.

If $n > 0$ the body of the algorithm is equivalent to "return the value of $n * \text{factorial}(n-1)$ as the value of factorial". If the algorithm is totally correct for the argument $n - 1$, then it is clearly totally correct for the argument n. QED

In the next to the last paragraph above, we have proved that the algorithm is correct for $n = 0$. In the last paragraph above, we have shown that if the algorithm is correct for $n = 0$, it is correct for $n = 1$. This, in turn, implies that it is correct for $n = 2$, etc. Thus it is correct for all non-negative integral values of the argument.

4.4. The value to be returned by the algorithm is not defined. If the algorithm is executed with such a value for the argument, it will never terminate. On most real systems, execution will stop and the system will issue an error message indicating that the stack has grown to occupy all available memory.

4.5. Data values can be sorted if they are elements of a set on which an ordering relation (sometimes called a "collating sequence" in business data processing) has been defined. I.e., if the values are in a linearly ordered set, it is meaningful to speak of sorting them. Examples are the set of numbers, the set of strings of some fixed length, the set of strings of variable length, etc.

4.6. Quicksort rearranges and subdivides the collection of values to be sorted (the sort keys) into two subcollections. One subcollection contains the lower key values in the original collection; the other subcollection, the higher keys. Quicksort calls itself recursively to sort each of the two smaller subcollections thus formed. See [Aho, section 3.5], [Knuth, Vol. 3, p. 114 ff.] and [Wirth, section 2.2.6].

4.7. Before designing the algorithm, it is useful to have an outline of its correctness proof in mind. From the general description of the sorting method (see answer to the preceding question), a proof by induction on the number of items to be sorted is an obvious choice. We will assume that our algorithm sorts collections of fewer than n keys and will construct it so that it will sort a collection of n keys. The fact that a collection containing zero or only one key is already sorted will provide a convenient starting point for the inductive proof.

The following algorithm will rearrange (permute) the values of the subscripted variables key(i), i = first, first + 1, ... last, so that they are in ascending sequence, i.e. so that

$$\text{key(first)} \leqslant \text{key(first} + 1) \leqslant ... \leqslant \text{key(last)},$$

provided that last − first + 1 ⩾ 0.

```
quicksort(key, first, last);
IF first ⩾ last
THEN return (The subarray contains 0 or 1 keys and is therefore
        already sorted.)
ELSE subdivide(key, first, last, mid)
        quicksort(key, first, mid − 1)
        quicksort(key, mid, last)
        return;
```

4.8. The algorithm subdivide must rearrange and subdivide the collection of keys to be sorted into two subcollections in such a way that each is smaller than the original and so that every key in one subcollection is less than or equal to every key in the other subcollection. The algorithm must further identify the boundary between these two subcollections.

These requirements can be stated more precisely as follows. When called with parameters (key, first, last, mid), the algorithm subdivide must permute the values of the subscripted variables $key(i)$, $i =$ first, first $+ 1$, ... last, and calculate a value of the variable mid so that

$$first < mid \leqslant last$$

and

$$\max(key(i), first \leqslant i < mid) \leqslant \min(key(i), mid \leqslant i \leqslant last).$$

Note that the above requirements imply that first $<$ last. The calling task must ensure that this condition is satisfied.

4.9. Proposition: If the algorithm quicksort (see the answer to question 4.7) is called with the parameters (key, first, last) and if last $-$ first $+ 1 \geqslant 0$, then it will terminate with

$$key(first) \leqslant key(first + 1) \leqslant ... \leqslant key(last).$$

Proof: Note that the number of keys in the collection to be sorted is given by the expression (last $-$ first $+ 1$). We will call the value of this expression n.

If the number of keys to be sorted is 0 or 1, then first $\geqslant$ last. In this case, the algorithm obviously terminates (it is equivalent to a null algorithm, returning having done nothing). The rest of the proposition is a null proposition which is, by definition, true.

We have shown that if the collection to be sorted contains fewer than two keys, the algorithm sorts it correctly. Next, we will show that if the algorithm sorts fewer than n keys, it will sort n keys, completing the proof by induction.

If there are two or more keys to be sorted, then first $<$ last. In this case, the algorithm is equivalent to

```
subdivide(key, first, last, mid)
quicksort(key, first, mid − 1)
quicksort(key, mid, last)
return
```

After the call to subdivide is executed, we have, by definition of that algorithm,

first $<$ mid $\leqslant$ last.

The number of keys to be sorted by the first call to quicksort is mid $-$ first. But $0 <$ mid $-$ first $<$ last $-$ first $+ 1 = $ n. The number of keys to be sorted by the second call to quicksort is last $-$ mid $+ 1$. But $0 <$ last $-$ mid $+ 1 <$ last $-$ first $+ 1 = $ n. I.e., each of these calls to quicksort requires that at least one but fewer than n keys be sorted.

If quicksort sorts fewer than n keys correctly, then we have, after the first call to quicksort,

$$\text{key(first)} \leqslant \text{key(first} + 1) \leqslant ... \leqslant \text{key(mid} - 1)$$

and after the second call to quicksort,

$$\text{key(mid)} \leqslant \text{key(mid} + 1) \leqslant ... \leqslant \text{key(last)}.$$

It is obvious that

$$\text{key(mid} - 1) \leqslant \max(\text{key(i), first} \leqslant i < \text{mid})$$

and

$$\min(\text{key(i), mid} \leqslant i \leqslant \text{last}) \leqslant \text{key(mid)}.$$

But, by definition of the algorithm subdivide,

$$\max(\text{key(i), first} \leqslant i < \text{mid}) \leqslant \min(\text{key(i), mid} \leqslant i \leqslant \text{last}),$$

which implies that key(first) $\leqslant ... \leqslant$ key(mid $- 1) \leqslant$ key(mid) $\leqslant ... \leqslant$ key(last). Thus, if quicksort sorts fewer than n keys (and $n \geqslant 2$), then quicksort also sorts n keys. We showed earlier that quicksort sorts 0 or 1 key. Therefore, it also sorts 2 keys, and therefore 3 keys, etc. QED

Note that in the above proof certain implicit assumptions have been made regarding the way variables and parameters are handled when the algorithms subdivide and quicksort are called. These mechanisms are outlined in the answer to exercise 4.1 above. To be mathematically precise and complete, however, we would have to specify in detail the effects upon the data environment of executing such calls to subsidiary algorithms.

4.10. At intermediate steps in the subdividing process, the algorithm will have formed three subcollections: one with low keys, one with high keys and the third with key values not yet assigned to either of the other two subcollections. Initially, the third subcollection will contain all key values; upon completion of the subdivision process, none. If the key variables to be subdivided are key(first), key(first + 1), ... key(last), then we may define internal variables il and ih such that

$$(\text{first} \leqslant i < \text{il}) \Rightarrow \text{key}(i) \text{ is in the set of low keys}$$

and

$$(\text{ih} < i \leqslant \text{last}) \Rightarrow \text{key}(i) \text{ is in the set of high keys.}$$

This will be our loop invariant. If ih < il, then every key is assigned to either the set of low keys or to the set of high keys, in which case the subdivision is complete. This will be the loop termination condition.

4.11. We begin by establishing the truth of the loop invariant. Writing the loop body so that the truth of the loop invariant is maintained and using the loop termination condition stated in the answer to the preceding question, we obtain the following algorithm:

```
subdivide(key, first, last, mid);
pivotindex ← any element of {first, first + 1, ... last};
pivotkey ← key(pivotindex);
il ← first; ih ← last;
WHILE il ≤ ih
DO BEGIN
    WHILE key(il) < pivotkey DO il ← il + 1;
    WHILE key(ih) > pivotkey DO ih ← ih − 1;
    ASSERTIONS: 1. il ≤ ih + 1,
                2. key(ih) ≤ pivotkey ≤ key(il);
    IF il = ih
    THEN IF il < (first + last)/2
            THEN il ← il + 1
            ELSE ih ← ih − 1
    ELSE IF il < ih
            THEN exchange the values of key(il) and key(ih),
                 il ← il + 1, ih ← ih − 1
            ELSE (empty);
    ASSERTIONS: 3. first < il,
                4. ih < last,
                5. il ≤ ih + 1;
END;
return the value of il as the value of mid;
```

Each condition in an ASSERTION statement is a proposition which is purported to be true at the point in the algorithm where it appears. These propositions will be used in the proof of the correctness of the algorithm. During execution of the algorithm, they are disregarded. (Some real computing systems evaluate assertions when the algorithm is executed. If one is found to be false, execution stops and an error message is issued.)

A more precise formulation of the loop invariant than the one given above is:

$$(\text{first} \leqslant i < \text{il}) \Rightarrow (\text{key}(i) \leqslant \text{pivotkey})$$

and

$$(\text{ih} < i \leqslant \text{last}) \Rightarrow (\text{key}(i) \geqslant \text{pivotkey}).$$

4.12. Proposition: When called with parameters (key, first, last, mid), where first < last, the algorithm subdivide (see the answer to question 4.11) alters the array key only by permuting the values of the variables key(i), i = first, first + 1, ... last, assigns a value to the parameter mid and terminates with

first < mid ⩽ last

and

$$\max(\text{key}(i), \text{first} \leqslant i < \text{mid}) \leqslant \min(\text{key}(i), \text{mid} \leqslant i \leqslant \text{last}).$$

Proof: We begin by noting that the initialization establishes the truth of the invariant of the main (outer) loop (see answer to exercise 4.11 above).

In order to prove that the two inner WHILE loops terminate, that assertions 1 through 5 are true and that the truth of the loop invariant is maintained, it is convenient to distinguish between the first and subsequent executions of the main loop:

Case A: first execution.

Initially, first = il < ih = last. In the first inner WHILE loop, il will be increased until key(il) ⩾ pivotkey. At the latest, this will occur when il = pivotindex. Thus, the loop will terminate with il ⩽ pivotindex. Similarly, the second inner WHILE loop will terminate with pivotindex ⩽ ih. Therefore, il ⩽ ih at assertion point 1 and assertion 1 is true.

The truth of assertion 2 follows directly from the exit conditions of the two inner WHILE statements.

The first inner WHILE statement adds key values less than pivotkey to the set of lower key values (by increasing il). The value of the variable il is increased from il0 to il1 = il0 + 1 if and only if key(il0) < pivotkey, maintaining the truth of the loop invariant. The second inner WHILE statement performs the corresponding function for key values greater than pivotkey and similarly maintains the truth of the loop invariant.

Consider the possible paths through the nested IF statements. The ELSE–ELSE path is executed if and only if il > ih. But as we showed above, il ⩽ ih, so execution cannot follow this path during the first execution of the body of the main loop.

We prove assertions 3 and 4 by contradiction. Assume that assertion 3 is false, i.e. first ⩾ il. Initially, il = first. No statement in the algorithm reduces the value of il, therefore il is always greater than or equal to first. Thus, il must be equal to first. The only paths through the nested IF statements which do not increase il are the THEN–ELSE and the ELSE–ELSE paths. The first of these is executed only if il ⩾ (first + last)/2, which implies that first ⩾ last. This contradicts the given condition that first < last. The second of these paths will not be followed during the first execution of the loop body as was shown above. Therefore, assertion 3 must be true.

Assertion 4 is proved in a similar manner. If assertion 4 is false, then ih = last. The only possible path through the nested IF statements which does not decrease ih is the THEN–THEN path. This path is taken only if il = ih and il < (first + last)/2, which together imply that first > last, a contradiction of the given condition. Therefore, assertion 4 is true.

Denote the values of il and ih at assertion point 1 by il1 and ih1 respectively. Denote the values of il and ih at assertion point 5 by il5 and ih5 respectively. By considering all possible paths through the IF statement, we have

$$(il1 = ih1) \Rightarrow \text{either } (il5 = il1 + 1) \text{ and } (ih5 = ih1)$$
$$\text{or } (ih5 = ih1 - 1) \text{ and } (il5 = il1)$$
$$\Rightarrow (il5 = ih5 + 1)$$

and

$$(il1 < ih1) \Rightarrow (il5 = il1 + 1) \text{ and } (ih5 = ih1 - 1)$$
$$\Rightarrow (il5 < ih1 + 1 = ih5 + 2)$$
$$\Rightarrow (il5 \leqslant ih5 + 1).$$

Since il1 $\leqslant$ ih1, this proves the truth of assertion 5.

In the following, we will denote the values of key(.) at assertion points 1 and 5 by key1(.) and key5(.) respectively. To prove that the nested IF statements also preserve the truth of the loop invariant, we consider the cases il1 < ih1 and il1 = ih1 separately.

If il1 < ih1, assertion 2 and the effect of the IF statement will ensure that

$$key5(il1) = key1(ih1) \leqslant pivotkey \leqslant key1(il1) = key5(ih1),$$

$$il5 = il1 + 1 \qquad \text{and} \qquad ih5 = ih1 - 1.$$

This adds key5(il1) = key5(il5 − 1) to the set of low keys and key5(ih5 + 1) to the set of high keys. Combining the above, we have

$$key5(il5 - 1) \leqslant pivotkey \leqslant key5(ih5 + 1),$$

i.e., the truth of the loop invariant has been maintained.

If il1 = ih1, key1(il1) = key1(ih1) = pivotkey. This key value may be added to either subcollection without violating the loop invariant.

The truth of the loop invariant is therefore maintained in all possible cases.

Case B: subsequent executions

After the body of the main loop has been executed the first time, first < il and ih < last (assertions 3 and 4). Because no statement in the algorithm decreases il or increases ih, these conditions will remain true at all subsequent times.

The first inner WHILE statement will cause il to be increased until key(il) $\geqslant$ pivotkey. The truth of the loop invariant at the beginning of the loop together with the truth of assertion 4 throughout the loop imply that ih + 1 $\leqslant$ last and key(ih + 1) $\geqslant$ pivotkey. Therefore, il will not be increased beyond ih + 1, i.e. the first inner WHILE loop will terminate with il $\leqslant$ ih + 1. The truth of the loop invariant will be maintained by the first inner WHILE statement (see proof for case A). Similarly, the second inner WHILE statement will terminate with il − 1 $\leqslant$ ih. This proves assertion 1.

As in case A above, the truth of assertion 2 follows directly from the exit conditions of the two inner WHILE loops.

Assertion 5 and the truth of the loop invariant may be proved as in case A above. Here, however, we must consider the additional possibility that il1 = ih1 + 1. The IF statement is equivalent to an empty statement, so assertion 5 follows from assertion 1.

Similarly, the truth of the loop invariant is maintained.
(End of case B.)

Because the body of the main loop is always executed at least once, assertions 3, 4 and 5 are true when the loop terminates. Then, assertion 5 and the WHILE exit condition imply that il = ih + 1. Because the final value of il is returned as the value of mid, we have

first < mid ⩽ last.

Upon termination, the loop invariant implies that

$$\max(key(i), first \leqslant i < mid) \leqslant pivotkey \leqslant \min(key(i), mid \leqslant i \leqslant last).$$

The only statement which changes the value of any of the variables key(.) is the statement which exchanges the values of key(il) and key(ih). As we have shown above, first ⩽ il and ih ⩽ last. The exchange statement is executed only if il < ih, so we have first ⩽ il < ih ⩽ last. The exchange takes place, therefore, within the range of subscript values specified in the proposition. Exchanging objects is, of course, a permutation and a series of permutations constitutes a permutation. Finally, if the exchange statement is never executed, that constitutes a permutation also (the identity permutation). Thus, the algorithm alters the array key only by permuting the values of the variables key(i), i = first, first + 1, ... last.

Therefore, the algorithm is partially correct. Examining all paths through the main loop, we see that the difference ih − il is decreased by at least one on each execution. The main loop will therefore terminate in finite time and the algorithm is totally correct. QED

A more formally structured proof of the correctness of quicksort and of a slightly different version of subdivide can be found in [Foley]. In that paper, the algorithm subdivide will, under certain circumstances, form a third subcollection containing one element equal to pivotkey.

It is interesting and enlightening to compare the above approach to designing this algorithm with the Mocsian approach: Build it and see if it collapses; if it does, keep patching it until it doesn't. The first try might look something like this:

```
subdivide(key, first, last, mid);
pivotindex ← any element of {first, first + 1, ... last};
```

```
pivotkey ← key(pivotindex);
il ← first; ih ← last;
WHILE il ≤ ih
DO BEGIN
      WHILE key(il) ≤ pivotkey DO il ← il + 1;
      WHILE key(ih) > pivotkey DO ih ← ih − 1;
      IF il < ih
      THEN exchange the values of key(il) and key(ih),
            il ← il + 1, ih ← ih − 1
      ELSE (empty);
      END
return the value of il as the value of mid;
```

Here, as before, the collection of keys to be sorted is divided into two subcollections. But now, the lower subcollection will contain keys less than *or equal to* pivotkey (note the ≤ in the first inner WHILE condition). All keys greater than pivotkey will be assigned to the higher subcollection.

After writing the above algorithm and reviewing it cursorily, the next step in the Mocsian approach is to "test" (try) it. The first error encountered is likely to result from the selection of the highest key in a small subcollection as pivotkey. In this case, the first execution of the first inner WHILE statement will cause il to "run off the end", i.e. to be incremented to a value higher than last. What actually happens afterward depends upon whether the subcollection being subdivided is the highest one or not and if it is, what values are in the array key beyond the entire collection of keys to be sorted. In any event, the observed symptoms of this error may very well be confusing; the programmer's attention will not necessarily be directed immediately to the cause of the problem.

This error, if found, will probably be "corrected" by changing the conditions in the two inner WHILE statements so that the variables il and ih cannot "run off the end":

WHILE il ≤ ih AND key(il) ≤ pivotkey DO ...

WHILE il ≤ ih AND key(ih) > pivotkey DO ...

The first correction is made because it is necessary; the second one is made to be "safe".

Problems can still arise if array subscripts are checked during run time. If il = ih + 1 and ih = last, a bounds array error may occur when evaluating the first WHILE condition above, even though the condition would evaluate to false. This error will occur only if the highest subcollection is being subdivided and the highest key in that subcollection is selected as pivotkey. Relatively few test cases will force this situation to occur. It is probably just as easy to construct a proper proof of correctness (and thereby discover all mistakes, not just one) as it is to determine the need for and construct such a test case.

After introducing the above change, the algorithm will be run again on the machine. Again, it may or may not terminate successfully. If the "test" is successful and signals the presence of the other mistake, the program will run until the stack has grown to occupy all available memory. The programmer will probably spend considerable time perusing dumps and/or listings of traces until he finds the reason – the algorithm will have repetitively divided some collection of n elements into two subcollections, one containing all original n elements and the other one empty.

This failure will occur only if the highest key in a subcollection is selected as pivotkey enough times to cause stack overflow. If pivotindex is selected randomly and a relatively large amount of memory is available for the stack, this is a rather unlikely event – unless all keys in the subcollection are equal, also a relatively uncommon situation. This is a good example of the kind of error which goes undetected during "testing", only to arise some time after the program is put into productive use and when the programmer is no longer available to find and correct his mistakes.

This error, due to a fundamental oversight in the design of the algorithm subdivide, will send the programmer "back to the drawing board". An obvious way to patch up the mistake is to add code at the end of the algorithm to check for this condition. When it arises, the highest element is located and exchanged with the last element and two subcollections of n − 1 and 1 elements returned. This is, of course, a rather inelegant way to circumvent the mistake. It also results in an unnecessarily inefficient algorithm.

It is also possible that the programmer will fail to find the cause of one of the above troubles. Especially a programmer with an inadequate foundation in basic principles is likely to be stumped by the last difficulty mentioned above. Understanding it presupposes an understanding of the method of inductive proof in mathematics. He might very well conclude that recursion may be fine in theory but obviously doesn't work in practice. Not having really believed in the first place that this method would work, he is not surprised that it doesn't, and is likely to attribute the failure to the method and not to his faulty application of it.

4.13. The following non-recursive version of quicksort calls the algorithms stack and unstack. Stack saves an ordered pair of values in a stack; unstack retrieves a pair of values from the stack. Each pair of values in the stack represents an interval of subscripts whose key values have not yet been sorted.

```
quicksort(key, first, last);
IF first ≥ last
THEN return (The collection to be sorted contains 0 or 1 key and is
therefore already sorted.)
ELSE stack((first, last))
      WHILE stack not empty
      DO BEGIN
            unstack((low, high))
            subdivide(key, low, high, mid)
            IF mid − low > 1 THEN stack((low, mid − 1));
            IF high − mid + 1 > 1 THEN stack((mid, high));
            END;
      return;
```

Note that the ELSE part of each IF statement within the WHILE loop is empty.

4.14. We will only outline the proof here. The loop invariant is:
1. each entry in the stack represents an interval of subscripts whose corresponding key values must be rearranged – within the interval – to complete the sort and
2. the value of a key whose subscript is not in an interval represented by an entry in the stack is in its final place.

The loop invariant and the WHILE exit condition (the stack is empty) together imply that sorting is complete.

Each execution of the body of the loop reduces the size of one interval in the stack (possibly replacing it by two smaller intervals). Because no entry in the stack represents an interval containing fewer than two key values, the algorithm will eliminate all stack entries, and therefore terminate, in finite time. This argument can be formalized by considering the sum over all intervals in the stack of a suitably chosen strictly convex function of the number of key variables in the interval (e.g. the square of this number). The value of this sum is reduced by at least a fixed amount each time the body of the loop is executed, therefore the value of this function will be reduced to zero in a finite number of steps. But a zero value of the sum implies that the stack is empty, i.e., that the algorithm terminates.

4.15. The report's format must fulfill the following criteria. Each printed page is correct when it contains
1. the header with page number,
2. at least one line of data,
3. if not the last page, at least a certain minimum number of lines of data,
4. at most a certain maximum number of lines of data and
5. the footer with the same page number as the header.

The report is correct when each page is correct, when no data group is separated onto two pages and when the pages are numbered consecutively beginning with a given first page number. The header and the footer must appear in exactly the same positions on every page. Note that if the report contains no data, neither a header nor a footer is to be printed.

It should also be noted that the above specifications imply an upper limit on the number of lines in a single data group. This maximum number of lines per data group and the minimum and maximum number of lines of data per page (specified in points 3 and 4 above) must be selected so that they are consistent with one another, i.e. so that the above specifications can always be met.

4.16. We define the global format control variables as follows:

Report page	Line number	Description
	1	first line
Header	...	
	11h	last line in header
	11h + 1	first line of data
Data	...	
	min1d	minimum last data line
	...	
	max1d	last data line
	max1d + 1	first line in footer
Footer	...	
	11p	last line on page

In addition, we define the following global variables:

Variable	Description
firstpage	the number of the first page
pageno	the current page number
lineno	the number of lines printed on current page

We require that the algorithm generating the data to be printed first call the algorithm "openprinting" to initialize printing, then call "printdatalines" as many times as needed and, finally, call "closeprinting" to end the report. The algorithms openprinting and closeprinting have no parameters. When openprinting is called, the printing mechanism must be physically positioned at the top line of the first page. After closeprinting is executed, the printing mechanism will be positioned at the top line of the page following the report just printed.

The algorithm printdatalines has the parameters (dataline, first, last) where dataline is an array of data lines and first and last are subscripts. The algorithm printdatalines will print the variables dataline(first), dataline(first + 1), ... dataline(last) on successive lines of the same page. The calling algorithm must ensure that last − first + 1 (the number of lines to be printed) does not exceed maxld − minld + 1 (the variability allowed in the number of lines of data on one page).

Our algorithms for printing a report are as follows:

```
openprinting;
pageno ← firstpage − 1
lineno ← llp
return;

printdatalines(dataline, first, last);
IF first > last THEN return (no data lines to print);
IF lineno ⩾ minld THEN newpage;
FOR i ← first TO last STEP 1
print(dataline(i))
lineno ← lineno + 1
NEXT i
return;

newpage;
IF pageno ⩾ firstpage THEN printfooter;
printheader;
return;

printheader;
pageno ← pageno + 1
print the header (llh lines with pageno)
lineno ← llh
return;

printfooter;
skiplines(maxld − lineno)
print the footer (llp − maxld lines with pageno)
return;

closeprinting;
IF pageno ⩾ firstpage THEN printfooter;
return;
```

The above algoriithms assume that

$$0 \leqslant \text{llh} < \text{minld} \leqslant \text{maxld} \leqslant \text{llp}$$

and that the algorithms print and skiplines exist. Calling print causes the argument to be printed on the next line of the report. Invoking skiplines with an argument $n \geqslant 0$ causes the printing mechanism to skip n blank lines on the page.

The effect of the algorithm print is probably most simply defined as follows:

```
print(datastring);
report(pageno, lineno + 1) ← datastring
return
```

where report is the name of an array. The value of the subscripted variable report(p, l) is the data appearing on line l of page p of the printed report. This way of expressing the print command illustrates that it (and any other input/output statement) is just a particular kind of assignment statement.

The effect of skiplines can be defined in a similar way:

```
skiplines(n);
FOR i ← 1 TO n STEP 1
report(pageno, lineno + i) ← blank line
NEXT i
return
```

The algorithm printdatalines above will print the minimum number of data lines on each page consistent with the specifications. If the second IF statement in printdatalines is replaced by

IF lineno + last − first + 1 > maxld THEN newpage;

then printdatalines will print the maximum number of data lines on each page permitted by the specifications.

The reader should verify in detail that these algorithms, called as specified above, will produce the correct results. Use the approach employed in the answers to the previous questions.

It is interesting to contemplate how many times in the last decades this "wheel has been reinvented" – incorrectly.

4.17. The following is the syntax of a number, using BNF notation:

⟨number⟩ ::= ⟨sign⟩ ⟨integer⟩ ⟨fraction⟩

   ⟨sign⟩ ::= ⟨empty⟩| +| −

 ⟨integer⟩ ::= ⟨digit⟩|⟨digit⟩ ⟨integer⟩

⟨fraction⟩ ::= ⟨empty⟩|.⟨integer⟩

   ⟨digit⟩ ::= 0|1|2|3|4|5|6|7|8|9|

4.18. The following is a state transition table for a finite automaton which will determine whether a given string satisfies the above syntactical definition of a number:

State	Description	Next character of string				
		+	−	digit	·	other
1	Start	2	2	3	E	E
2	Sign	E	E	3	E	E
3	Digit	E	E	3	4	E
4	Digit.	E	E	5	E	E
5	Digit . digit	E	E	5	E	E
E	Error	E	E	E	E	E

The string satisfies the syntactical definition of a number if and only if the automaton is in state 3 or state 5 after scanning the entire string.

An algorithm for simulating the finite automaton is given below. This algorithm returns either "true" or "false" as its value depending upon whether or not the value of its argument is a syntactically correct number or not. It is assumed that the array nextstate contains the above data and that the value of the variable correctfinalstates is a set consisting of the states 3 and 5.

```
syntaxcorrect(string);
state ← 1
FOR pos ← 1 TO length(string) STEP 1
state ← nextstate(state, character(string, pos))
```

NEXT pos
return the value of (state IN correctfinalstates) as the value of syntaxcorrect

It is assumed that the function length(string) returns the length of the string in character positions and that character(string, pos) returns the character in position pos of string.

4.19. The following is a tabular definition of a finite automaton which will generate the abbreviation of a given string of letters. The upper entry in each position of the table is the character to be appended to the partially formed output abbreviation. (Where a blank appears, no character is to be appended.) The lower entry in each position of the table is the next state. The automaton starts in state 1 and with an empty output string:

State	Next character of input string																									
	A	B	C	D	E	F	G	H	I	J	K	L	M	N	O	P	Q	R	S	T	U	V	W	X	Y	Z
1	A	B	C	D	E	F	G	H	I	J	K	L	M	N	O	P	Q	R	S	T	U	V	W	X	Y	Z
start	2	3	3	3	2	3	3	3	2	3	3	3	3	3	2	3	3	3	3	3	2	3	3	3	2	3
2		B	C	D		F	G			G	C	L	M	M		B	Q	R	C	D		V	V	X		Z
vowel	2	3	3	3	2	3	3	2	2	3	3	3	3	3	2	3	3	3	3	3	2	3	3	3	2	3
3	A				E				E						O						U				E	
cons.	2	3	3	3	2	3	3	3	2	3	3	3	3	3	2	3	3	3	3	3	2	3	3	3	2	3

The algorithm to simulate this finite automaton is a minor modification of the algorithm given in the answer to question 4.18:

```
abbreviation(name);
state ← 1
abb ← the null string
FOR pos ← 1 TO length(name) STEP 1
abb ← abb + output(state, character(name, pos))
state ← nextstate(state, character(name, pos))
NEXT pos
return the value of abb as the value of abbreviation;
```

In the above algorithm, "+" stands for the string concatenation operator. It is assumed that the values of the elements of the arrays output and nextstate are as given in the table above.

The reader is invited to compare this definition of the algorithm with a conventional program for generating the abbreviation.

4.20. We will use the structure of a finite automaton for specifying the control logic for the recommendation process. The state of the automaton will be one of the data items in each article's data record. The "input" to the automaton will be the event that has occurred:

ord: order placed
time: time for automatic cancellation
crinor: criterion for normal recommendation satisfied
criurg: criterion for urgent recommendation satisfied
week: time for weekly summary to be printed

If, during any one daily or weekly processing run, more than one of the above applies to any one article, the events are processed in the above order. The "output" from the automaton will be a command to execute one of the following actions:

record: record open order
cancel: issue notice of automatic time cancellation
ordnor: calculate and record recommended reorder quantity
prturg: print urgent recommendation
pwdate: print on weekly summary and record date for automatic cancellation
pws: print on weekly summary without modifying recorded date for automatic cancellation

The following table defines the behaviour of the control mechanism. The upper entry in each position of the table specifies which action (if any) is to be performed. The lower entry specifies the next state.

State	Event				
	ord	time	crinor	criurg	week
0 no rec.	record 0	0	ordnor 1	0	0
1 not pr.	record 0	1	ordnor 1	prturg 3	pwdate 2
2 weekly	record 0	cancel 0	2	prturg 4	pws 2
3 daily	record 0	3	3	3	pwdate 5
4 w/d	record 0	4	4	4	pws 5
5 d/w	record 0	cancel 0	ordnor 6	5	pws 5
6 d/w part	record 0	6	ordnor 6	6	pwdate 5

As mentioned earlier (see the answer to question 2.3), it can sometimes be shown that a given finite automaton is equivalent to another with fewer states. In the actual situation from which this exercise was derived, the interviews with the user led originally to an automaton with 18 states. The designers had little difficulty in reducing that automaton to the above one with only 7 states.

4.21. If the variable DATA-A in MODA behaves as an own variable, the following will be displayed:

MAIN PROGRAM
1
MODULE B
2

If, however, the variable DATA-A in MODA behaves as a local variable, non-existent between the return from and the next call to MODA, the following will be displayed:

MAIN PROGRAM
1
MODULE B
1

If DATA-A in MODA is an own variable, the value "2" will be retained from one activation (call) of MODA to the next. If DATA-A in MODA exists only locally, the second call of MODA will cause DATA-A to be recreated. The VALUE phrase will ensure that it is initialized to "1" upon recreation.

If no overlaying occurs, DATA-A in MODA will behave as an own variable. It will exist throughout the activation time of the entire program of which MODA is a part. If MODA and MODB are overlaid, then the variable DATA-A ceases to exist when MODB is called and loaded. When MODA is called the second time, it must be reloaded, in which case DATA-A is initialized to "1" because of the VALUE phrase.

In many real COBOL systems, a variable declared in the working storage section of an overlaid module may sometimes be treated as an own variable and sometimes as a local variable, depending upon whether the module in question was in fact reloaded or not. For example, if MODA and MODB were overlaid and if the calls in the main program were changed to:

CALL "MODA".
CALL "MODA".
CALL "MODB".
CALL "MODA".

then the following would be displayed by most systems:

MAIN PROGRAM
1
2
MODULE B
1

Between the first and second calls to MODA, no reloading is necessary and DATA-A behaves as an own variable. The value "2" of DATA-A is retained between the calls to MODA. Calling MODB causes overlaying; the variable DATA-A ceases to exist, thus behaving as a local variable. The third call to MODA causes it to be reloaded and DATA-A to be recreated and initialized to the value "1".

The inconsistent treatment of such local/own variables by some real systems can lead to what appears to be erratic behaviour during execution. It can and often does confuse programmers, especially less experienced ones. It also means that the program code itself is ambiguous – obviously an undesirable situation. The parameters and control statements specifying how the program is to be linked and loaded complement the program code; only this combination defines unambiguously the behaviour of the program.

Concurrent execution of computational tasks

5.1. The criteria for the correctness of the algorithm are:

1. The value assigned to the variable available(flight) by one computational task must be the value of that variable when first accessed (i.e. when evaluating the IF condition) less the value of the variable seatsdesired input from the keyboard associated with that task.
2. When several requests for seats on one flight are made more or less simultaneously, they must be processed in such a way that the final value of available(flight) is equal to the initial value of that variable less the sum of all requests honored.

In order to satisfy the first criterion above, it is essential that the value of available(flight) not be changed by another task between the two fetching references to this variable made by a task executing the proposed algorithm. In order to satisfy the second criterion above, it is essential that no other task reference (fetch the value of or assign a new value to) the variable available(flight) between the times this variable is first referenced and the newly calculated value is assigned to it. The latter requirement is more restrictive.

The given algorithm does not enforce either of the above conditions and hence will not, in general, yield correct results when executed in an environment permitting concurrent task execution. Whether the results are erroneous or not in any particular case depends upon the sequence in which the various statements in the several tasks' algorithm(s) are actually executed. The sequence in which such statements are actually executed in a typical real multitasking system depends upon a great many factors, most of them beyond the control of any one task. The sequence of execution is seldom reproducible; for all intents and purposes it can be considered to be random.

The following examples illustrate some of the problems which can arise if the conditions stated above are violated. Both tasks are executing the proposed algorithm. It is assumed that the same flight has been selected by both tasks and that initially 5·seats are available.

Example 1:

task 1	task 2
seatsdesired ← 3	
IF 3 ⩽ 5	
	seatsdesired ← 4
	IF 4 ⩽ 5
THEN available ← 5 − 3 = 2	
	THEN available ← 2 − 4 = −2

In the above example, the flight has been overbooked despite the fact that the proposed algorithm checks for and attempts to prevent over-booking. The reservation status is correct and reflects the overbooking.

Example 2:

task 1	task 2
seatsdesired ← 3	
IF 3 ⩽ 5	
	seatsdesired ← 4
	IF 4 ⩽ 5
THEN (evaluating) 5 − 3 = 2	
	THEN (evaluating) 5 − 4 = 1
THEN available ← 2	
	THEN available ← 1

In each task, the assignment statement in the THEN part of the IF statement has been interrupted after evaluating the right hand side and before the new value has been assigned to the variable available(flight). In this case, 7 seats have been sold but the reservation file indicates that 1 seat is still available. In effect, the sale of 3 seats in task 1 has not been recorded.

The solution to these problems is suggested by the second criterion for correctness given above. We must add a statement to our algorithm which reserves access to the variable available(flight) for the executing task exclusively. Any subsequence reference to this variable by another task (including another request to reserve access) will cause the execution of that other task to be suspended until the variable is no longer reserved. The revised algorithm is:

flight ← flight identification input from keyboard
seatsdesired ← number input from keyboard
reserve(available(flight))
IF seatsdesired ⩽ available(flight)
THEN available(flight) ← available(flight) − seatsdesired
ELSE display message that seats are not available
release (available(flight))

The release statement cancels the effect of the reserve statement, allowing other tasks to reference the previously reserved variable.

In many systems, the above function "reserve" is called "lock" because it "locks out" attempts by other tasks to reference the variable. Some systems provide a combined operation which reserves and fetches the value of a variable (often called "read with lock") and another combined operation which stores a new value of and releases a variable (often called "rewrite and unlock").

The reader should prove that the above algorithm is partially correct (that it meets the criteria specified above) and that it always terminates.

5.2. The use of the reserve statement (see the answer to the preceding question) can cause the execution of other tasks to be suspended, possibly indefinitely, as shown by the following example:

task 1	*task 2*
reserve(x)	
	reserve(y)
reserve(y) (task suspended)	
	reserve(x) (task suspended)

Here, task 1 is suspended because it has attempted to reference the variable y, which has already been reserved by task 2. Task 1 will remain suspended until task 2 releases the variable y.

Similarly, task 2 is suspended because it has attempted to reference the variable x, which has already been reserved by task 1. Task 2 will remain suspended until task 1 releases the variable x.

But neither task 1 nor task 2 can proceed to a later release statement as long as it is suspended. Thus, task 1 cannot proceed until task 2 proceeds and task 2 cannot proceed until task 1 proceeds. Therefore, neither will ever proceed. This situation is often called a "deadlock".

Any number of tasks can be involved in a deadlock situation. For example, task 1 can block task 2, which in turn blocks task 3, ..., which in turn blocks task n, which in turn blocks task 1. The reference which causes suspension need not be a reserve statement; any "locked out" reference will suffice.

In proving that an algorithm will always terminate when executed in a multitasking environment, one must ensure that no reference to any variable can result in an indefinite suspension of the referencing task. To avoid the possibility that a task causes a deadlock by reserving access to some variable, the programmer must be able to prove that after executing a reserve statement, a task will proceed to the corresponding release statement in finite time, regardless of the action and effects of other tasks.

5.3. Deadlock can be prevented only by following a suitable convention for reserving variables when designing algorithms to be executed concurrently. Any one of several conventions may be followed for reserving common variables (variables not local to a task), for example:

Convention 1: All common variables to be referenced during and between the execution of a reserve statement and the corresponding release statement are reserved in a single reserve statement. (If any such variable is already reserved by another task, the system will suspend the reserving task until all requested variables can be reserved for it.) When the computation is finished, one or more release statements executed by the reserving task release all variables previously reserved. Each algorithm is written in such a way that a second reserve statement will never be executed until all reserved variables have been released. It is clear that, if such a convention is followed, execution of an algorithm cannot be prevented from proceeding to the release statement by reservation conflicts. Therefore, any task which has reserved variables will release them in finite time; a deadlock cannot occur.

Convention 2: An ordering of all common variables is defined. All common variables accessed by a task are reserved individually in the defined order. When access is no longer required, each reserved variable is released by the task which reserved it. More precisely, common variables are reserved and released in such a way that whenever a variable x is to be reserved by task t,

1. every lower variable which will be referenced in the subsequent sequence of executed statements ending with the release of x is already reserved by the task which will reference it and
2. no higher variable is reserved by task t.

This implies that no deadlocked situation can occur. (The reader should work out a detailed proof of this proposition, identifying clearly all assumptions which must be made. Hint: Prove by contradiction. Assume that a set of tasks suspended because of attempts to reserve variables forms a deadlocked situation. Show that one of these tasks is not blocked by any other task in the deadlocked set, in contradiction of the assumption.)

One must ensure that the rules of the selected convention are not violated by execution paths involving more than one task. Consider, for example, the following algorithms following convention 2 with the ordering (a, b, c, d):

Algorithm A:

    reserve a
    reserve c
    activate task using algorithm B,
            suspending self until termination
    release c
    release a
    terminate task;

Algorithm B:

    reserve b
    reserve d
    ...
    release d
    release b
    terminate task;

The sequence of execution is:

Task 1   *Task 2*

reserve a
reserve c
        └──────┐
              reserve b
              reserve d
              ...
              release d
              release b
       ┌──────┘
release c
release a

This sequence of reserving the variables (a, c, b, d) violates the convention (the variable b has not been reserved by task 2 when the variable c is reserved by task 1). Mutual blocking with another task which reserves the variables in the order (a, b, c, d) is possible. A comparable example can be constructed for convention 1.

If algorithm A above is modified to:

Algorithm A':
    reserve a
    reserve c
    activate task using algorithm B,
            not suspending self until termination
    release c
    release a
    terminate task;

then the execution of the activating task continues concurrently with that of the activated task and the sequence of execution is:

reserve a
reserve c

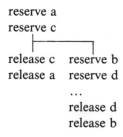

release c   reserve b
release a   reserve d

      ...

      release d
      release b

In this case, convention 2 is not violated and no deadlock can occur with other tasks also following the convention. After reserving variables a and c, algorithm A′ will always release them. Similarly, once variables b and d are reserved, algorithm B will proceed to the corresponding release statements. With regard to reservation of variables, we have two independent tasks, in contrast to the first example above in which the two tasks were sequentially linked.

One must distinguish between deadlock and the more general situation in which some task is indefinitely suspended. By deadlock, we mean a situation in which two or more tasks mutually prevent each other from proceeding because of the manner in which they have reserved common variables or other system resources (such as input/output devices, memory, etc.). A task can remain suspended for an indefinite length of time for other reasons as well.

No matter what convention is followed, certain prerequisites must be fulfilled in order to guarantee that deadlock cannot occur and that any suspended task will eventually proceed. Perhaps most importantly, any task which reserves a variable must proceed to the corresponding release statement if given access to all variables as required. (Otherwise, it could reserve a variable and then go into an infinite loop, perhaps blocking other tasks indefinitely.) If the task's algorithm terminates, then this condition is obviously fulfilled.

In general, it is possible that new tasks can be continually activated (created) and executed in such a way that they keep certain variables continuously reserved, thereby preventing indefinitely a suspended task from proceeding. Such possibilities can be eliminated by suitable priority schemes in the multitasking operating system or by limiting the rate at which new tasks may be activated to something less than the capacity of the actual system to execute them. Results of queuing theory are of relevance to these considerations.

Computer arithmetic

6.1. No. The field axioms require, among other things, that both operations are associative and commutative and that the distributive laws hold. Floating point addition as normally implemented is not associative. For example, if a floating point scheme represents numbers with 6 decimal digits of accuracy and rounds, then evaluating $(1234560 + 4) + 4$ will yield 1234560 but $1234560 + (4 + 4)$ will result in 1234570. If the system truncates instead of rounding, then evaluating $(1234560 + 5) + 5$ will yield 1234560 but $1234560 + (5 + 5)$ will result in 1234570.

Many other properties of a field do not apply in floating point arithmetic systems. For example, $(x + y = x) \Rightarrow (y = 0)$ in a field, but for many values of x and any y in a certain neighborhood of 0, $x + y = x$ in floating point arithmetic systems. Similarly, there exist values of x and y with y not equal to 1 but with $x * y = x$.

A floating point system as usually implemented consists, in effect, of a function f from a bounded subset B of the real numbers onto a finite subset F of the intersection of B and the rational numbers. For every x in F, the function maps a neighborhood of x (in B) into x. The operations floatadd and floatmul are usually defined as follows:

$$\text{floatadd}(x, y) := f(x + y)$$

$$\text{floatmul}(x, y) := f(x * y)$$

for all x and y in F. The function f would be a homomorphism of $(B, +, *)$ onto $(F, \text{floadadd}, \text{floatmul})$ if and only if for all x and y in B

$$\text{floatadd}(f(x), f(y)) = f(x + y) \text{ and}$$

$$\text{floatmul}(f(x), f(y)) = f(x * y).$$

But by definition of floatadd and floatmul

$$\text{floatadd}(f(x), f(y)) = f(f(x) + f(y)) \text{ and}$$

$$\text{floatmul}(f(x), f(y)) = f(f(x) * f(y)).$$

It does not follow from the definitions above (and it is not generally true) that $f(f(x) + f(y)) = f(x + y)$ and $f(f(x) * f(y)) = f(x * y)$. I.e., (F, floatadd) is not a group, (F, floatadd, floatmul) is not a field and the function f does not exhibit the main characteristic of a homomorphism. Therefore, it is not surprising that floating point arithmetic operations fail to exhibit many of the "nice" properties of normal arithmetic. Floating point arithmetic on typical computer systems is very useful, but one must be careful not to expect too much from it.

For further information on floating point arithmetic, see [Knuth, Vol. 2, section 4.2].

6.2. This behaviour is not surprising. The system undoubtedly involves approximate arithmetic, as a result of which the associative law does not hold. (See the answer to question 6.1.)

Probably, non-decimal (e.g. binary) representation is employed by the machine. The binary representation of .01 (decimal) is a repeating fraction. When truncated or rounded, precision and accuracy of decimal fractions may be lost.

Computational complexity

7.1. By the complexity of an algorithm we mean the way in which the amount of time, memory space or some other computational resource required during the execution of the algorithm grows as the size of the problem to be solved increases. Depending upon the resource of interest we speak of time complexity, space complexity, etc. If, for example, an algorithm sorts n items in $c * n^2$ seconds, where c is some positive number, then we say that the time complexity of the sorting algorithm is $O(n^2)$ ("the order of n squared"). The asymptotic behaviour of the relationship between time and size of problem (the number of items to be sorted) is usually of paramount interest, not the exact amount of time required to execute the algorithm for a particular set of input data. See [Aho], [Brady] and [Schnorr].

The order of a function is defined mathematically as follows. A function f(n) is said to be of the order of g(n), written $f(n) = O(g(n))$, if there exist numbers h and m such that $|f(n)/g(n)| < h$ for all $n > m$.

7.2. If the a priori probability that key(i) = searchkey is the same for all values of i, the time complexity of this linear search algorithm is O(n), where n = end − start + 1, the number of items to be sorted. For many other probability distributions, including the worst possible case, the time complexity is also O(n).

This can be shown by considering L, the number of times the loop is executed before the algorithm terminates. If p is the probability that searchkey appears in the table, the expected value of L is given by

$$E(L) = p * (n + 1)/2 + (1 - p) * n$$
$$= n * (1 - p/2) + p/2$$
$$= O(n)$$

Each execution of the loop takes, we will assume, approximately the same amount of time. The total time required is then $c1 + c2 * L$, where $c1$ and $c2$ are some positive numbers. The expected time is therefore $c1 + c2 * E(L) = O(n)$.

The searching time is longest when key(end) = searchkey or when searchkey is not in the table at all. In these cases, the expected execution time is also O(n).

7.3. Proposition: The time complexity of the binary search is O(log(n)), where n = end − start + 1, the number of items in the table to be searched.

Proof: Let il{i} and ih{i}, i = 1, 2, ..., represent the values of the variables il and ih respectively at the beginning of the i-th execution of the loop. The initialization sets il{1} = start and ih{1} = end. We further define s{i} := ih{i} − il{i} + 1, the number of items still to be searched. Note that s{1} = n.

Each execution of the body of the loop either locates searchkey (in which case the algorithm terminates) or reduces the value of s{.} to half of its previous value or less as we will show below. After calculating a new value for ip in the i-th execution of the loop,

$$ip = integer\big((il\{i\} + ih\{i\})/2\big) \Rightarrow$$

$$ip \leqslant (il\{i\} + ih\{i\})/2 < ip + 1.$$

If, after the body of the loop has been executed the i-th time, searchkey has not been located, then either

a. $il\{i+1\} = ip + 1$ and

$ih\{i+1\} = ih\{i\}$

or

b. $il\{i+1\} = il\{i\}$ and

$ih\{i+1\} = ip - 1$

Case a leads to

$$s\{i+1\} = ih\{i+1\} - il\{i+1\} + 1$$
$$= ih\{i\} - ip$$
$$\leqslant (ih\{i\} - il\{i\} + 1)/2 = s\{i\}/2.$$

Case b leads to

$$s\{i+1\} = ih\{i+1\} - il\{i+1\} + 1$$
$$= ip - il\{i\}$$
$$< (ih\{i\} - il\{i\} + 1)/2 = s\{i\}/2.$$

Therefore, $s\{i+1\}/s\{i\} \leqslant 1/2$ and $s\{m\}/s\{1\} \leqslant (1/2)^{(m-1)}$. In particular, if $m = \text{integer}(\log(n) + 2)$, where log means the logarithm to the base 2, we have

$$s\{m\} < s\{1\}/n = 1.$$

But $s\{.\}$ is an integer, therefore $s\{m\} \leqslant 0$. This implies that $ih\{m\} < il\{m\}$, which in turn implies that the loop terminates. Therefore, the loop will be executed at most $\text{integer}(\log(n) + 1)$ times and the algorithm is of time complexity $O(\log(n))$. QED

7.4. The time required to perform a binary search increases as $\log(n)$, while the time required to perform a linear search increases linearly with n, i.e. much faster than $\log(n)$. Therefore, if very large tables are to be searched, the binary search will be completed sooner than the linear search, no matter how slow the computer used for the binary search and no matter how fast the computer used for the linear search.

More precisely, for any given slow computer executing the binary search algorithm and any given fast computer executing the linear search algorithm, there exists a critical table size (number of table entries). The slow computer executing the binary search will search any larger table faster than the fast computer executing the linear search will search that same table.

7.5. Each entry in the stack represents an interval of at least two items to be sorted; the intervals do not overlap. Therefore, the number of entries in the stack is at most $n/2$, where n is the number of items to be sorted. The space complexity is, therefore, $O(n)$.

The maximum possible number of entries will be stored in the stack if the algorithm subdivide always splits the collection of key values such that one subcollection contains exactly two items and the other, the rest. In the great majority of cases, the expected number of entries in the stack will be less. The expected space complexity depends upon the method used to select pivotindex but is typically $O(\log(n))$.

Data structure

8.1. A sequential file is a sequence of data elements or groups of data elements. Each term in the sequence is called a record. During the execution of an algorithm, the records in the file must be accessed in the order in which they appear in the sequence. Skipping forward or backward is not permitted. Usually, additional restrictions are placed on changing the value of a data element in a sequential file.

8.2. A relative file is an array or a group of arrays. One dimension of the subscript of every array in the relative file takes on values in a common set I, the set of "record numbers". Usually I is a finite set of consecutive integers beginning with 0 or 1.

8.3. An index for an array x is a table. Each entry in the table contains a data value d and a subscript value s such that $x(s) = d$. For every subscript i, the value of $x(i)$ appears in the table.

An index is usually stored in the form of one or more arrays. Typically, the entries in the index are stored in an order which facilitates searching the index, for example, using the binary search algorithm (see question 7.3).

More precisely, an ordered index for the array x with subscripts in I is the pair of arrays (key, loc) with subscripts in a common, linearly ordered set S, with

key(r) $\leqslant$ key(s) for all r $\leqslant$ s in S,

key(s) = x(loc(s)) for all s in S and

for every i in I there exists an s in S with loc(s) = i.

The value of loc(s) is a "pointer" to the value of key(s) in the array x.

While not strictly necessary, it is usual to require, in addition to the above, that no duplicate entries appear in the index, i.e., that loc(r) = loc(s) only if r = s. Then the index is, in effect, a permutation of the values of the subscripted variables x(.). It sorts the array x.

From the standpoint of informational content, the array key in the above definition is redundant and may be omitted. Only if key(s) can be accessed significantly faster than x(loc(s)) is it advantageous to maintain the array key.

8.4. An indexed file, as usually implemented, is a relative file for which one or more indices are available. Included in an indexed file system are algorithms which, given the value and the array name of a data element, use the appropriate index to determine the value(s) of the subscript and the values of the other array variables with the same subscript. Also included are algorithms for adding entries to and deleting entries from the file and its indices.

8.5. An inverted file is an indexed file for which an index exists for every array in the file.

8.6. A hierarchical index is a multilevel index. The table constituting the complete index (see the answer to question 8.3 above) is split into sections of convenient size. An index to these sections is prepared; this second level index contains one entry for each section of the complete, lower level index. The second level index is, in turn, split into sections and a (third) index to these sections is constructed in the same manner. Higher level indices are constructed repeatedly until the highest level index is no larger than one section in size.

8.7. Indices are structured hierarchically for reasons of efficiency of searching, inserting new entries and deleting entries.

If the entries of an index are ordered and stored in consecutive locations of a memory space, the index can be searched in $O(\log(n))$ time, e.g. using the binary search algorithm (see question 7.3). But each insertion and each deletion requires moving, on average, half of the index. This requires $O(n)$ time. Various tricks may be used to postpone the need to move part of the index, e.g. placing new entries into "overflow" areas, "deleting" entries by marking them but leaving them in place, etc. But sooner or later, either such an index must be "reorganized", which causes the insertion and deletion time to increase as $O(n)$, or else the searching time ultimately requires $O(n)$ time.

If an index is structured hierarchically and a suitable algorithm is used for placing a new record in the relative file (i.e., for assigning values to a group of array variables with a previously unused value for the common subscript), the times required for searching, inserting and deleting increase only as $O(\log(n))$. Detailed analyses of hierarchical indices (also called trees), their use and maintenance can be found in [Knuth, Vol. 3, sections 6.2.2–6.2.4].

Program structure

9.1. The terms modular programming, structured programming, top-down programming and hierarchical programming refer, in their narrow sense, to an approach to designing, structuring and writing programs. More generally, the approach is equally applicable to the design of algorithms for software systems of any size – consisting of many programs or of only a part of a program.

No one universally accepted definition of any of these terms exists, but generally, they refer to a design approach or philosophy based on the following guidelines [Brooks, pp. 143–144], [McGowan]. A software system should be subdivided into a relatively small number of subsystems, each of which is also subdivided into a small number of subdivisions, etc., until the level of individual program statements is reached. Each subunit, or module, should be small enough that it can be understood easily by a human reader. It should be small enough that the interrelationships among its individual parts (program statements, calls to subsidiary modules, etc.) can be clearly seen. It should be large enough to perform a significant function. It should perform only one or a small number of closely related functions. The interactions between any one module and other modules should be simple and well defined. Each module should have only one entry point and should return control only to the point in the superior module from which it was called. In some situations in a multitasking environment, a return may not be appropriate at all, in which case the algorithm should simply terminate. Only one exception to this guideline is often condoned: if an error condition arises which precludes the module from performing its function (a "fatal" or "catastrophic" error), the module may transfer control to another module which abnormally terminates the program run.

These guidelines imply that GO TO statements, if present at all, should transfer control only to statements within the module in which they appear. They also imply that related routines should not be in one module, but should form separate modules which call each other as necessary.

The term structured programming is also used by some people in a more restricted sense: a structured program is a program in which only the IF ... THEN ... ELSE ... and the WHILE ... DO ... structures are used to modify the normal sequence of execution of program statements. In this sense, the term structured programming is often considered to be synonymous with "GO TO-less programming". Purists argue that the GO TO should be prohibited completely, while others relax this requirement and propose that the GO TO statement should be used only to form clearly and simply structured loops. In any event, all professional programmers agree that the GO TO should be used carefully, discriminately, within a short range and only with good reason.

9.2. The greatest advantage claimed for this approach is that it leads to a software system exhibiting an increased simplicity of organizational structure, control structure and internal communication. As a result, the process of designing the system can be carried out more easily. The system design will, it is claimed, contain fewer errors than when a more traditional approach is employed. Furthermore, errors can be detected and corrected more easily, either by human review of the program listing or by testing (to the extent possible – see the questions on testing below). Perhaps most importantly, the correctness of each module can be more easily proved formally using appropriate mathematical methods. By restricting the size of the module as outlined in the answer to question 9.1 above, one restricts in turn

- the complexity of the procedure the human is expected to review and comprehend,
- the number of combinations of input values, and hence the number of test cases, which must be run during the test and
- the complexity of the correctness proof.

The separation of the quicksort algorithm into the main control module (quicksort) and the module for rearranging the values to be sorted (subdivide) is a good example of this (see the answers to questions 4.6–4.14).

The hierarchical organization of units of limited size is a technique which has been in widespread use by mankind for many purposes over a time span of many thousands of years. Almost all social, political and economic organizations are so structured. Physical structures, machines, etc., are similarly structured. An automobile, for example, is not designed as a conglomerate of several thousand parts; it is designed as a combination of a few major subassemblies (engine, chassis, body, etc.), each of which is made up of a few subunits, etc. A building, a bridge, an airplane, computer hardware – all have always been designed and structured in this same way. Mathematical proofs are similarly structured: a complex proof of a theorem is typically subdivided into simpler proofs of subsidiary theorems, lemmata, etc. It is surprising that some two decades passed before a major fraction of software system designers and programmers recognized that this approach is also applicable to the structures they build.

9.3. Various rules of thumb have been proposed for the size of a module, such as one half to one page, between five and fifty program statements, no more than n IF statements, no more than one loop, etc. While these rules of thumb are sometimes useful in specific contexts, the general guidelines stated in the answer to question 9.1 above should take precedence. Comprehensibility and reduction of logical complexity, both within the module and in its interfaces with other modules, are the main goals.

9.4. The specification and documentation of a single module must identify the input data variables used and must contain a definition of the module's output. Any assumptions about relationships among the values of the input variables (input assertions or propositions) should be explicitly stated. The definition of the module's output will usually take the same form (output assertions or propositions). Finally, the functional relationship between the module's inputs and its outputs must be explicitly defined, unless, of course, it is implied by the output assertions.

Mathematically, a module's algorithm maps the data environment as it exists at the point in time when the module is invoked (called, activated) into another data environment. The module's function must, therefore, be specified completely and unambiguously just as any other mathematical function. Its domain and range must be specified as well as the way in which the value of the function is to be determined from the value of its argument. Part of the specification of the domain and the range are the input and output assertions, which serve to restrict the defined domain and range to subsets of the set of all possible data environments involving the input and output variables.

The specification should include a reference to subsidiary modules and their input and output assertions as appropriate.

The proof of correctness of the module's algorithm should also be included in its documentation. If the proof is relatively simple, an outline of it may suffice; otherwise, it should appear in full. The proof can be of considerable value to another programmer who, sometime in the future, will be called upon to add features to the module.

Because many data elements are referenced, in general, by more than one module, it is usually best to define the data elements in a separate document. The specification and documentation of any one module will refer to the relevant sections of the documentation of the data.

The use of higher level programming languages and of hierarchical structures in programs has rendered the flow chart largely unnecessary for documentation purposes. Only occasionally will it be appropriate to include one in the documentation of a module. If a flow chart seems to be required, the designer should review his work carefully; in all likelihood, the module in question is logically too complex and should, therefore, be further subdivided.

The above comments apply only to the documentation of a single module intended to be read by members of the development and maintenance teams. Other important documentation must be prepared for the system as a whole and for other readers, of course. For further information on the types of documentation required, see [Brooks, chapter 15] and [Kimm, chapter 4].

Testing

10.1. Two purposes exist for testing software. Frequently, the author of the program wants, subconsciously at least, to demonstrate that his program is correct, i.e. that it contains no errors ("bugs"). While this is an understandable goal, it is an improper reason for conducting a test.

Experience shows that almost all pieces of software contain errors. Usually, non-trivial software of any size initially contains many errors. The proper purpose of testing is to demonstrate the presence of errors and, hopefully, to localize or even identify them.

10.2. Employing the method of "black-box" testing, the tester constructs test cases based on the specifications of the module to be tested and runs the module with them as input. He is not permitted to look at the program code, i.e. he is not permitted to consider how the module operates internally [Myers].

10.3. Employing the method of "white-box" testing, the tester constructs test cases based on the specifications and the program code of the module. I.e., he is allowed to "look inside" the module when deciding what test cases should be run [Myers].

10.4. The correctness of a module can be demonstrated by black-box testing only by executing the module with every possible combination of values of the input variables. For all but the most trivial modules, this is totally impractical because the number of possible combinations is so large. For many modules, it is in fact impossible because the number of possible combinations is infinite. Of relevance in this connection is E. W. Dijkstra's famous comment that testing can show the presence, but never the absence, of errors in software [Buxton, p. 21, p. 85].

10.5. In general, the correctness of a module cannot be demonstrated by white-box testing any more than by black-box testing. Using the method of white-box testing, the tester usually attempts to construct a set of test cases which will cause all paths through the module to be executed. For a limited number of test cases, this approach is usually more likely to uncover an error in the module than black-box testing. It cannot be guaranteed, however, that a white-box test will uncover all errors (unless, of course, all possible combinations of inputs are tried).

In connection with white-box testing an interesting question arises: If the tester is to take the time to analyze the module's code in order to specify a large number of test cases, why doesn't he apply correctness proof methods to the code at the same time? If he were to do so, he would, in all likelihood, be able to prove the absence of errors or to identify some – probably in less time than it takes him to test the module and achieve less conclusive results.

Some project managers use a variation of this idea for its psychological and, hopefully, educational effect upon the programmer. After a module is programmed, they ostensibly construct test cases using the white-box approach. Actually, they try to construct a correctness proof; in the process, obstacles to the proof are found which represent errors in the code. Having identified the error(s), they construct test cases which will demonstrate the presence of those error(s). The programmer is then asked to run the test cases and to correct any errors which may turn up. To the extent that the programmer learns more by finding his errors himself, rather than by having them pointed out to him by the project manager, this approach has some merit. It is not, of course, the most efficient way of correcting the errors found by the project manager.

10.6. Practical guidelines for deciding when to stop testing depend upon the goals of the particular development project. Assuming that minimization of overall costs is the goal, testing should be stopped when the effort required to find succeeding errors is more costly than the expected consequences of leaving them undetected. Such a decision depends strongly, of course, on how serious the consequences of a software failure are likely to be and on the probability that another error will, in fact, ever turn up. In some cases, these decision parameters may be estimated reasonably accurately, but more often they can only be estimated subjectively. A variety of more specific rules for implementing the above general guideline have been proposed. See, for example, [Myers, pp. 122-128].

Some purists would propose that testing be stopped before it is started and that other methods be used for convincing oneself that the software is correct (or still contains errors). While there is much to be said for this suggestion, some minimum amount of testing will undoubtedly always be necessary.

One should distinguish between two very different aspects of "testing" as it is typically practiced in software construction today: trial and error design (a la Moc) vs. verifying that a completed piece of work meets specifications. Testing of the first type, while quite common today, is rarely, if ever, appropriate or necessary. Testing of the second type is appropriate and has its place in software engineering, just as it does in other engineering fields. But in the case of this type of testing, the object to be tested is expected, more often than not, to meet specifications when testing begins. Today, in the software field, this expectation is seldom fulfilled.

Project management

11.1. This project manager has an uncontrollable project. The only thing he can control is the expenditure of programmer resources. He cannot monitor progress sufficiently precisely to enable himself to recognize the need for corrective measures in time. The planning unit – all programs assigned to one programmer – is much too coarse.

The proposed method for estimating progress typically leads to estimates of the fraction of work completed which increase as originally planned until a level of about 80%–90% is reached. The programmers' individual estimates then increase only very slowly until the task is actually completed. Delays do not become evident, therefore, until the planned completion date is very near. Then, there is not enough time to take corrective action.

It is essentially impossible for the programmer to estimate the fraction of the program completed. What is 45% of a program? Worse yet, what is 45% of three programs? How is he to guess whether a program is 40% or 50% complete? The easiest way for the programmer to estimate such a figure is to divide the amount of time actually spent on the task to date by the time budgeted for that task. Only when the program is almost finished or when the allocated time budget is almost used up will he be able to recognize that the calculated figure is wrong. Thus, for much of the project's planned duration, the biweekly reports will be nothing more than an echo of the original plan. They will not reflect actual progress.

Thus, this project manager cannot control the results achieved during the project, but only at its end, when it is too late to take corrective action. He intends to and can verify that time is booked to the project as planned. There is, therefore, a significant danger that time actually spent on other work will be booked to this project, especially if other project managers control the value received more closely.

11.2. The basic planning unit ("activity" in project management jargon) should be smaller. Each activity should be an identifiable piece of work, defined in such a way that at any time it is obvious whether it has not yet been started, started but not yet completed or completed. No activity should require a large fraction of any resource for its execution; if a proposed activity does, it should be further subdivided.

The project manager should begin by subdividing the project into activities – individual programs, groups of modules or individual modules, each of which can be completed by one programmer in no more than a few weeks. Designing each program should probably be an activity separate from the coding of the individual modules, at least for the more complex programs. Testing each larger program should also be a separate activity, as should testing the system as a whole. Preparation of some parts of the documentation will constitute one or more activities. Other sections of the documentation will be produced within other activities as appropriate.

At the end of each reporting period (one week would probably be better than two weeks), each programmer should report the amount of time he has spent on each activity during the period. He should estimate how much more time he will need to complete each activity on which he worked during the period. If appropriate, in his opinion, he should also reestimate the time required to complete any other activity.

Shortly after the project has started, some activities should be completed. If they are not, the project manager should find out why and take appropriate action. Based on a comparison of estimated and actual times required to complete the first activities, he may find it desirable to revise the project plan and recalculate completion dates. Such review of the progress of the project should be an ongoing effort for which the project manager must reserve an appropriate amount of his time. This time should also appear in the project plan.

Good project management cannot guarantee that there will not be deviations from the plan, of course, but it will ensure that the project manager will recognize such deviations as soon as possible. He will be able to identify their probable effects on target dates, milestones, etc. long before any of these have been missed.

11.3. The first thing that such a project manager should do is to realize that the desired completion date may be unrealistic. Then, he should consider alternatives to his plan; perhaps he can find a realistic one which will enable him to complete the project earlier.

If he has not already done so, he should construct a PERT plan for the project as currently planned. After determining the critical path, he should consider alternative sequences of activities which move activities from the critical path to paths with slack.

He can also, of course, consider assigning more resources to activities on the critical path, thereby reducing the elapsed time required to complete the activities in question. His estimates of the resources required should take realistic account of communication and coordination overhead and similar effects. (If two men can do a job in two months, it is not necessarily true that four can do the same job in one month, particularly if it takes the two newcomers three months to learn what has to be done. The reader is referred to [Brooks, chapter 2] for a particularly elucidating and interesting exposition of such effects.)

Other important aspects of managing a group of programmers are discussed in [Weinberg].

In closing

12.1. In your view, the detailed specification, design and development of computer software is
a. a science or an engineering discipline
b. an art
c. a craft
d. a trade
e. a racket.

Bibliography

[1] ACM Ad Hoc Committee on Self-Assessment, "A Self-Assessment Procedure", Communications of the ACM, Vol. 19, No. 5, May 1976, pp. 229–235.

[2] ACM Committee on Self-Assessment, "Self-Assessment Procedure II", Communications of the ACM, Vol. 20, No. 5, May 1977, pp. 297–300.

[3] ACM Committee on Self-Assessment, "Self-Assessment Procedure III", Communications of the ACM, Vol. 20, No. 9, September 1977, pp. 621–624.

[4] Aho, Alfred V.; Hopcroft, John E.; Ullman, Jeffrey D., "The Design and Analysis of Computer Algorithms", Addison-Wesley Publishing Co., Reading, Massachusetts, 1974.

[5] Arbib, Michael A., "Theories of Abstract Automata", Prentice-Hall, Inc., Englewood Cliffs, N.J., 1969.

[6] Brady, J.M., "The Theory of Computer Science: A Programming Approach", Chapman and Hall, London, 1977.

[7] Brooks, Frederick P. Jr., "The Mythical Man-Month", Addison-Wesley Publishing Co., Reading, Massachusetts, 1979.

[8] Buxton, J.N.; Randell, B. (editors), "Software Engineering Techniques, Report on a conference sponsored by the NATO Science Committee, Rome, Italy, 27th to 31st October 1969", NATO Science Committee, Brussels, 1970.

[9] Dahl, O.-J.; Dijkstra, E.W.; Hoare, C.A.R., "Structured Programming", Academic Press, London, 1972.

[10] Dreyfus, Hubert L., "What Computers Can't Do; The Limits of Artificial Intelligence", Harper & Row, New York, 1979.

[11] Evans, Christopher, "The Micro Millennium", Washington Square Press Pocket Books, New York, 1981.

[12] Fairley, Richard E., "Software Engineering Education: Status and Prospects", Proceedings of the Twelfth Hawaii International Conference on System Sciences, Pt. I, pp. 140–146, Western Periodicals Ltd., North Hollywood, California, U.S.A., 1979.

[13] Foley, M.; Hoare, C.A.R., "Proof of a recursive program: Quicksort", The Computer Journal, Vol. 14, No. 4, November 1971, pp. 391–395.

[14] Harrison, Michael A., "Introduction to Switching and Automata Theory", McGraw-Hill Book Company, New York, 1965.

[15] Kimm, Reinhold; Koch, Wilfried; Simonsmeier, Werner; Tontsch, Friedrich, "Einfuehrung in Software Engineering", Walter de Gruyter & Co., Berlin, 1979.

[16] Knuth, Donald E., "The Art of Computer Programming, Volume 1, Fundamental Algorithms", Addison-Wesley Publishing Co., Reading, Massachusetts, second edition, 1978.

[17] Knuth, Donald E., "The Art of Computer Programming, Volume 2, Seminumerical Algorithms", Addison-Wesley Publishing Co., Reading, Massachusetts, 1969.

[18] Knuth, Donald E., "The Art of Computer Programming, Volume 3, Sorting and Searching", Addison-Wesley Publishing Co., Reading, Massachusetts, 1973.

[19] Manna, Zohar, "Mathematical Theory of Computation", McGraw-Hill Kogakusha, Ltd., Tokyo, 1974.

[20] McGowan, Clement L.; Kelly, John R., "Top-Down Structured Programming Techniques", Petrocelli/Charter, New York, 1975.

[21] Minsky, Marvin L., "Computation: Finite and Infinite Machines", Prentice-Hall, Inc., Englewood Cliffs, N. J., 1967.

[22] Myers, Glenford J., "The Art of Software Testing", John Wiley & Sons, New York, 1979.

[23] Naur, Peter (editor), "Revised Report on the Algorithmic Language Algol 60", Regnecentralen, Copenhagen, 1962.

[24] Naur, Peter; Randell, Brian (editors), "Software Engineering, Report on a conference sponsored by the NATO Science Committee, Garmisch, Germany, 7–11 October 1968", NATO Scientific Affairs Division, Brussels, 1969.

[25] Royden, H. L., "Real Analysis", The Macmillan Company, Collier-Macmillan Limited, London, second edition, 1970.

[26] Schnorr, C.P., "Rekursive Funktionen und ihre Komplexitaet", B.G. Teubner, Stuttgart, 1974.

[27] Schulz, Arno, "Methoden des Softwareentwurfs und Strukturierte Programmierung", Walter de Gruyter, Berlin und New York, 1978.

[28] Statistisches Bundesamt, "Statistisches Jahrbuch 1980 fuer die Bundesrepublik Deutschland", W. Kohlhammer GmbH, Stuttgart und Mainz, 1980.

[29] U.S. Bureau of the Census, "Statistical Abstract of the United States: 1979" (100th edition), Washington, D.C., 1979.

[30] Weinberg, Gerald M., "The Psychology of Computer Programming", Van Nostrand Reinhold Company, New York, 1971.

[31] Weizenbaum, Joseph, "Computer Power and Human Reason; from Judgment to Calculation", W.H. Freeman and Co., San Francisco, 1976.

[32] Wiener, Norbert, "The Human Use of Human Beings; Cybernetics and Society", Doubleday and Co., Inc., Garden City, N.Y., 1954.

[33] Wirth, Niklaus, "Algorithms + Data Structures = Programs", Prentice-Hall, Inc., Englewoods Cliffs, N.J., 1976.

[34] Zinsser, H., "Rats, Lice and History", Little, Brown & Company, Boston, Massachusetts, 1935.

Colophon

The manuscript of this book
was transferred to the publisher
by the Author
in the form of a machine-readable copy
prepared with a Tandy TRS 80 system
and transmitted via a dial-up telephone line to
a DECSYSTEM 2060 and subsequently converted to
a Harris 7400 photocomposer,
both of these at
Northprint, Meppel, the Netherlands,where also the desk-editorial
corrections were implemented,
as made from Amsterdam in remote-control mode
by Arie Jongejan.
The book is type-set in
Times New Roman 10/12
and was produced by Geoffrey Andrew.
Its cover is the work of the publisher's resident artist,
Jan de Boer,
using a Han Kruyswijk photograph
of Miss Jenske Dijkhuis.
Published by
the North-Holland Publishing Company
March MCMLXXXII.